TOP**10**
SEATTLE

Top 10 Seattle Highlights

The Top 10 of Everything

CONTENTS

Seattle Area by Area

Streetsmart

The rapid rate at which the world is changing is constantly keeping the DK Eyewitness team on our toes. While we've worked hard to ensure that this edition of Seattle is accurate and up-to-date, we know that opening hours alter, standards shift, prices fluctuate, places close and new ones pop up in their stead. So, if you notice we've got something wrong or left something out, we want to hear about it. Please get in touch at **travelguides@dk.com**

Welcome to
Seattle

The largest city in Washington State, Seattle is known for its innovation, ambition, and creativity – after all, it is the birthplace of industry giants such as Amazon and Starbucks. Beyond this, the city is home to bustling markets, engaging museums, and diverse neighborhoods, and is encircled by dense forests and soaring mountains. With DK Eyewitness Top 10 Seattle, it's yours to explore.

Spectacular scenery surrounds the city. To the west of downtown's skyscrapers are the waters of **Puget Sound** and the snowy peaks of the **Olympic Mountains**. From the observation deck in **Columbia Center** or the **Volunteer Park Water Tower**, you can admire the **Cascade Mountains** in the east. The city itself is made up of seven different neighborhoods, each with its own distinct character, including **Capitol Hill's** vibrant LGBTQ+ scene, **Ballard's** celebration of its Scandinavian roots, and **West Seattle's** beachy vibe.

Seattle is an effervescent mix of the old and the new. The totem pole in **Pioneer Square** bears testament to the rich heritage of the area's Indigenous peoples, while the funky bars and shops on **Broadway** embrace millennial subcultures. Steeped in tradition, the 100-year-old **Pike Place Market** continues to sell produce to eager shoppers, while the striking architecture of the **Central Library** and the glassy globes of the **Amazon headquarters** propel the city into the future.

Whether you're coming for a weekend or a week, our Top 10 guide brings together the best of everything that Seattle has to offer, from intriguing museums and idyllic urban retreats to local dive bars and farm-to-table restaurants. The guide has useful tips throughout, from seeking out what's free to finding off-the-beaten-path spots, plus seven easy-to-follow itineraries, designed to tie together a clutch of sights in a short space of time. Add inspiring photography and detailed maps, and you've got the essential pocket-sized travel companion. **Enjoy the book, and enjoy Seattle**.

Clockwise from top: **Sunset over Bell Harbor Marina, totem pole in Pioneer Square, flower stalls at Pike Place Market, West Point Lighthouse, Space Needle in Seattle Center, Museum of Pop Culture, Washington Park Arboretum and Japanese Garden**

Exploring Seattle

Using downtown Seattle as a base, it is easy to reach the city's top attractions on foot or via public transit. A few of them are in the outer neighborhoods, all readily accessible by bus, but the freedom of a car for the day may be enjoyable. Keeping orientated is easy – the waters of Puget Sound will always be to the west.

Museum of Pop Culture
Space Needle
SEATTLE CENTER
Discovery Park
4 miles (6 km)
BUS 33
2
Olympic Sculpture Park
3
BELLTOWN

The heart and soul of the city, Pike Place Market is a historical landmark that promises a gastronomical adventure.

Key
— Two-day itinerary
— Four-day itinerary

Two Days in Seattle

Day ❶
MORNING
Visit the stalls at **Pike Place Market** (see pp12–13), and enjoy theatrically-prepared fare at the Pike Place Fish Market. Grab a cup of coffee at the original Starbucks store located here.

AFTERNOON
Ride the monorail from Westlake Center to **Seattle Center** (see pp14–15) for a trip up the iconic Space Needle. Afterwards, record a future hit single at the Museum of Pop Culture.

Day ❷
MORNING
Meet the wildlife that lives in Puget Sound at the Seattle Aquarium then shop for souvenirs along the **Seattle Waterfront** (see pp16–17) before sitting down for a seafood lunch.

AFTERNOON
Go underground in **Pioneer Square** (see pp18–19) to learn the history of Seattle's early settlers. Above ground, admire the Tlingit totem pole found in the small triangular square.

Four Days in Seattle

Day ❶
MORNING
Take a stroll in the historic grounds of the **University of Washington** (see pp28–9). Visit the Henry Art Gallery on campus for contemporary art and stop at the Washington Park Arboretum (see p45).

AFTERNOON
Capitol Hill (see pp78–85) is Seattle's hottest bar and restaurant district and the heart of Seattle's LGBTQ+ population. Fuel up with coffee, then catch a live show or dance at one of the neighborhood's inclusive clubs.

Day ❷
MORNING
Head down to **Discovery Park** (see pp32–3) for a refreshing hike and spectacular views of the Olympic Mountains. The expansive park is kept in a natural state to provide a peaceful respite from city life.

AFTERNOON
In summer and fall, stop at the Fish Ladder on **Lake Washington**

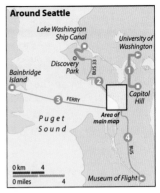

Pioneer Square features a replica of a carved cedar totem pole – a reminder of the area's Indigenous history.

for some window shopping and an ice cream, then plan the return trip to Seattle in time for sunset.

Day ❹
MORNING
Seattle was once called Jet City for its airplane industry. Visit the barn where Boeing made its first plane at the **Museum of Flight** (see p41).
AFTERNOON
Sip flavorful brews at Panama Hotel Tea & Coffee House in the **Chinatown-International District** (see pp22–3), the heart of Seattle's Pacific Rim culture. There are Vietnamese, Cambodian, and Chinese options for dinner, as well as pizza places and popular cafés.

Ship Canal (see pp26–7) to watch the salmon fight their way upstream. Watch fishing vessels share the water with kayakers in the Ballard Locks.

Day ❸
MORNING
Check out the impressive pieces in the **Olympic Sculpture Park** (see p17) on Seattle's waterfront, then spend a couple of hours browsing the world-class collection of global art at the **Seattle Art Museum** (see pp30–31).
AFTERNOON
Ride a ferry to **Bainbridge Island** (see p65). Walk into the village of Winslow

Seattle Art Museum has statues of guards from ancient Chinese tombs.

Top 10 Seattle Highlights

The futuristic Space Needle standing
tall above the Seattle skyline

🔟 Seattle Highlights

Seattle is a powerhouse of influence, pushing the country – and world – forward with the latest developments in technology, software, music, visual art, and, of course, coffee. It has emerged as one of the most ambitious cities in the United States, with a thriving downtown that has one of the nation's largest residential populations.

① Pike Place Market

An integral part of the Seattle experience, this market is famous for its mix of fresh seafood, farmers' produce, and variety of cuisines *(see pp12–13)*.

② Seattle Center

This center is dedicated to the pursuit of arts and entertainment. It's home to various sights, including the world-famous Space Needle and Gehry's Museum of Pop Culture, as well as the vibrant Chihuly Garden and Glass *(see pp14–15)*.

③ Seattle Waterfront

The city is a major port for both industrial and passenger traffic. Along with the Seattle Aquarium, sights include shops and restaurants just blocks from cranes loading containers *(see pp16–17)*.

④ Pioneer Square

A treasure trove of Victorian-era buildings and streets paved with cobblestones, Seattle's original commercial center was established in 1852 when Arthur A. Denny and David Denny arrived with fellow pioneers *(see pp18–19)*.

⑤ Chinatown-International District

The heart of Seattle's Asian American communities, this neighborhood *(see pp22–3)* has historic sights, restaurants, and more.

6 Broadway
Lined with cool bars, artworks, and indie stores, Broadway *(see pp24–5)* is the main street of the vibrant residential neighborhood of Capitol Hill.

Lake Washington Ship Canal 7
Officially completed in 1934, the canal bisects the city and provides access to the sea for pleasure boaters, research vessels, and commercial barges alike *(see pp26–7)*.

8 University of Washington
One of the nation's top universities, UW is home to more than 46,000 students and a campus. It's supported by endowments from benefactors in the tech industry *(see pp28–9)*.

9 Seattle Art Museum
Seattle's largest art museum is a treasure trove of fine art from around the globe. Its permanent collection includes Native American, European, and African works *(see pp30–31)*.

10 Discovery Park
Rising above Puget Sound is a gorgeous 534-acre (216-ha) park. Densely wooded trails, beaches, historic military homes, and wildlife are just some of its attractive features *(see pp32–3)*.

⭐ # Pike Place Market

First established in 1907, America's oldest farmers' market has become one of Seattle's most treasured institutions. The historic spot stretches for several blocks close to the waterfront, and includes a multilevel underground arcade, and street-level tables and stalls. By the mid-20th century, most stalls were run by Japanese Americans, and their tragic internment during World War II nearly ended the market's operation. Plans to raze the site fortunately ceased in 1971, when architect Victor Steinbrueck and his supporters saved it from the wrecking ball.

① Flower Stalls

The market's flower stalls **(below)** are largely owned by members of Seattle's small South East Asian Hmong community. The freshly picked blossoms can be smelled even before seeing them. In winter, residents make do with colorful dried flowers.

② Pike Place Fish Market

Market visitors and movie crews gather to witness these entertaining fishmongers **(above)**. Their skills include hurling their stock high over customers and counters.

③ Starbucks

Steamed, frothy milk and dark roasted coffee can now be found all over the world. Howard Schultz's retail coffee empire began right here in 1971, when Starbucks opened its first store.

NEED TO KNOW

MAP J4 ▪ Between Pike & Virginia St, from 1st to Western Ave ▪ (206) 682-7453 ▪ www.pikeplace market.org

Open daily, except Christmas & Thanksgiving

Flower Stalls: (425) 346-9691

Pike Place Fish Market: 86 Pike Pl; (206) 682-7181; www. pikeplacefish.com

Starbucks: 1912 Pike Pl; (206) 448-8762; www.starbucks.com

First and Pike News: 93 Pike St; (206) 624-0140

DeLaurenti: 1435 1st Ave; www.delaurenti.com

▪ **Three Girls Bakery** located on 1514 Pike St offers fresh bread and delicious sandwiches.

6 Buskers

Street music is a constant feature of market life. Visitors may catch the hyperkinetic show of a spoons player, who has featured in at least one award-winning rock video; or be entertained by gospel quartets, piano troubadours, or a clarinet soloist **(left)**.

RACHEL THE PIG

Be sure not to miss Rachel, Seattle's largest piggy bank. This brassy icon of the Market Foundation also serves as the market's sentry at the main entrance. All proceeds from visitors' donations to Rachel go toward low-income community groups.

Pike Place Market

8 Underground Mezzanines

Follow a maze of ramps and stairways to reach this shopping wonderland. Browse the books and collectibles, pay a visit to the palm reader, commission a portrait, or buy local arts and crafts as souvenirs.

9 Hillclimb

This enclosed stairway and elevator connects the market to the waterfront and more stores and restaurants in between. It also offers enchanting, far-reaching sea-to-mountain views.

7 Victor Steinbrueck Park

The wonderful grassy hill **(below)** here makes this park a popular lunch destination. Pack a picnic and admire the gorgeous views of Puget Sound, the Olympic Mountains, and the city's skyline.

10 DeLaurenti

Step inside this Mediterranean gourmet grocery to sample some of its delicious offerings. Combine its fresh breads, cheeses, and large wine selection to create a great summer picnic.

4 Farmers Market

Sample the freshest produce and specialty foods of Washington's organic farmers at the always popular outdoor Farmers Market, held daily from June through November. Stalls are located at various spots around downtown.

5 First and Pike News

This quaint, old-fashioned newsstand offers a wide array of newspapers and magazines from around the world. The stand has been here since 1979.

TOP 10 ⭐ Seattle Center

The site of the 1962 Century 21 Exposition, "America's Space Age World's Fair," Seattle Center has thrived through decades of growth all around it. The main attraction is still the Space Needle, though a close second is the Gehry-designed Museum of Pop Culture, Paul Allen's monument to rock music. The International Fountain also attracts throngs of visitors. The Center is the site of lavish presentations of art, theater, dance, and music all year long.

1 Seattle Children's Theatre (SCT)

Some 220,000 patrons are entertained by the SCT (above) each year. The Charlotte Martin and Eve Alvord theaters are known for their family-orientated programs.

3 Chihuly Garden and Glass

Bright, organic shapes made by internationally renowned glass sculptor Dale Chihuly sparkle in three distinct settings: museum installations, a glass house, and a garden (right).

Seattle Center

4 Museum of Pop Culture

Co-founder of Microsoft and rock enthusiast, Paul Allen commissioned the distinguished modern architect Frank Gehry to design this technicolor exhibition and perform-ance space (below). It is also home to the Science Fiction and Fantasy Hall of Fame (see p38).

5 Bumbershoot

Seattleites mark their calendars for the long Labor Day holiday weekend in September, when Bumbershoot (see p62) brings imaginative literary arts programs, artists, independent films, musicians, visual arts, delicious food, and many other surprises to Seattle Center.

2 McCaw Hall

The luxurious McCaw Hall (see p52) is home to the Seattle Opera and Pacific Northwest Ballet. The site also contains a café.

8 Pacific Science Center

Visitors will find exhibits on topics such as electronic music-making, robotics, hydraulics, and natural history **(left)** highly entertaining and informative. There are two IMAX theaters and an area for toddlers.

6 Seattle Center Monorail

Planners of the 1962 World's Fair imagined this as the future of mass transit *(see p39)*. The monorail makes the 1-mile (1.6-km) trip between here and downtown every ten minutes.

7 Armory

This large building houses the wonderful Seattle Children's Museum *(see p50)* as well as a theater, cafés, restaurants, and shops.

9 Space Needle

This imposing structure **(left)** is the city's architectural icon *(see p38)*. Ride the external elevators to the observation deck for a superb view, or sip wine at the bar, which has a revolving glass floor.

10 Seattle Repertory Theatre

"The Rep" *(see p52)* presents both contemporary as well as classic plays on its two stages: the Bagley Wright and Leo K. theaters.

1962 WORLD'S FAIR

The fair's designers demonstrated their vision of the future in 1962. Modernity ruled, from the science-fiction-esque Space Needle and monorail to the Sputnik-like Center Fountain. Nearly 10 million visitors came to marvel at this ideal future, and even Elvis Presley made an appearance, filming *It Happened at the World's Fair* (1963). Today, it is considered strictly retro, if not a little kitsch.

NEED TO KNOW

MAP H1–H2 ▪ (206) 684-7200 ▪ www. seattlecenter.com

Seattle Children's Theatre (SCT): 201 Thomas St; (206) 441-3322; www.sct.org

McCaw Hall: (206) 733-9725; www. mccawhall.com

Chihuly Garden and Glass: open 10am–5:30pm daily (to 6pm Fri–Sun); www.chihulygardenand glass.com

Museum of Pop Culture: (206) 770-2700; www. mopop.org

Seattle Center Monorail: (206) 905-2620; www. seattlemonorail.com

Pacific Science Center: (206) 443-2001; www. pacificsciencecenter.org

Space Needle: (206) 905-2100; opening hours vary, check website; www.spaceneedle.com

Seattle Repertory Theatre: (877) 900-9285; www.seattlerep.org

▪ Head to Queen Anne Ave for dining options.

TOP 10 ⭐ Seattle Waterfront

One of Seattle's most distinguishing features is its waterfront. The core of the city's thriving maritime community, it is full of the sights, sounds, and smells of a seaport metropolis. It is the place to catch ferries to the Kitsap Peninsula or Bainbridge Island, or to visit the Seattle Aquarium. The piers are tourist hotspots, replete with restaurants and bars, shops, and harbor tours. Sculptures by well-known modern artists fill the nearby Olympic Sculpture Park.

Seattle Aquarium ①

The waterfront's most popular all-weather attraction is the world-class Seattle Aquarium. Make a point of stepping inside the aquarium's glass-domed room under 400,000 gallons of water for spectacular views of sharks and octopuses.

SEATTLE MARITIME FESTIVAL AND THE TUGBOAT RACES

One of Seattle's most famous summer festivals *(see p62)*, this exciting event features the world's largest tugboat (a high-powered work boat) races on Elliot Bay.

② Cruise Ship Terminals

Seattle's proximity to Alaska's stunning Inside Passage, coupled with trends in leisure travel, led the city to build two terminals to accommodate the thousands of passengers. Watch ships docking at Bell Harbor Marina all summer long.

③ Ye Olde Curiosity Shop

Looking for literature etched on rice grains, or other unique objects? Since 1899, this has been the place to find curios, both from the distant and recent past **(above)**. It also sells a selection of coastal Native American art.

7 Olympic Sculpture Park

At the southern end of Myrtle Edwards Park, this space has views of Olympic Mountain and Puget Sound, and sculptures by Alexander Calder, Ellsworth Kelly, Jaume Plensa (left), and others.

Seattle Waterfront

4 Washington State Ferries

In addition to transporting commuters, these ferries (see p110), an icon of the Pacific Northwest, offer a picturesque and inexpensive cruise across Puget Sound.

5 Adventurous Activities

Adrenaline-seekers can strap on a paraglider and enjoy aerial city views. Kayak, boat, and paddle board rentals are also available.

6 Bell Harbor Marina

This harbor (below) provides moorage for pleasure boats (large and small). It is adjacent to the cruise-ship terminal.

8 Suquamish Museum, Bainbridge Island

Set in Port Madison on Bainbridge Island, this museum preserves cultural and historical artifacts from the Suquamish Indian Tribe, Seattle's original Indigenous residents. It welcomes visitors with tours, galleries, and rotating exhibits.

9 Seattle Great Wheel

For spectacular views of the city, a 20-minute spin on Seattle's Great Wheel (see p71) is a must. The 175-ft- (53-m-) tall structure has 42 gondolas and is perched over Elliott Bay.

10 Myrtle Edwards Park

Visit this waterfront haven (below) for fine views of Mount Rainier, Puget Sound, and the Olympic Mountains. A bike trail and pedestrian path winds along the Elliott Bay coastline.

NEED TO KNOW

MAP H4–5

Seattle Aquarium: Pier 59; (206) 386-4300; open 9:30am–6pm daily; closed Thanksgiving & Christmas; adm; www.seattle aquarium.org

Ye Olde Curiosity Shop: Pier 54; (206) 682-5844; open summer: 9am–9:30pm daily, winter: 10am– 6pm Sun–Thu, 9am–9pm Fri & Sat; www. yeolde curiosityshop.com

Washington State Ferries: Pier 52; (206) 464-6400; www.wsdot.wa.gov

Olympic Scultpure Park: 2901 Western Ave; (206) 654-3100; open daily; www.seattleart museum.org

Suquamish Museum, Port Madison: 6861 NE South St (ferry to Bainbridge Island); (360) 394-8499; open 10am–5pm daily; www.suquamish.nsn.us

Seattle Great Wheel: (206) 623-8607; open summer: 10am–11pm Sun– Thu (to midnight Fri & Sat), winter: hours vary; adm; www.seattle greatwheel.com

TOP 10 ⭐ Pioneer Square

The birthplace of modern Seattle has a colorful history marked by economic and geological fluctuations. The Great Fire of 1889 virtually destroyed it, before Alaska's Gold Rush breathed new life and Victorian architecture into the mix. Old warehouses were transformed into loft apartments and artist studios in the 1980s and 1990s. In 2001, the Nisqually earthquake caused structural damage. While rents have skyrocketed and developers continue to renovate the facades of relic buildings, the galleries, cafés, and entrepreneurial spirit remain.

4 Pioneer Square

This cobblestone triangle of recreational land, bordered by Yesler Way and First Avenue, is notable for its Tlingit totem pole, and its statue of Seattle's namesake, Chief Sealth *(see p37)*. The square also features an iron-and-glass pergola **(left)**, a replica of the original dating back to 1909, which once marked the entrance to the "finest underground restroom in the United States". Historic street lamps complete the old-world feel of the park.

1 First Thursdays

On the first Thursday of each month, from 5pm to 10pm, galleries sponsor an art walk *(see p62)*. Patrons can talk directly to the artists about their work. Start the tour on Occidental Way.

3 Skid Road

Henry Yesler's logging mill, used for sliding timber down to the wharf, sat at the foot of what is now known as Yesler Way. When an economic downturn hit in 1893, Skid Road came to signify desolation.

2 Last Resort Fire Department Museum

Housed in a fire station since 1928, this museum has the Pacific Northwest's largest collection of uniforms, antique fire apparatus, and vintage fire engines.

5 Merchants Cafe and Saloon

Popular and prospering since 1890, Seattle's oldest restaurant and bar **(below)** boasts a colorful past. Today, it dishes up hearty fare amid its little-changed Victorian decor.

NEED TO KNOW

MAP K5

Last Resort Fire Department Museum: 301 2nd Ave S; (206) 783-4474; open 11am–3pm Thu; www.lastresortfd.org

Merchants Cafe and Saloon: 109 Yesler Way; (206) 467-5070; open 11am–11pm Sun–Thu, (to 2am Fri & Sat)

Bill Speidel's Underground Tour: 614 1st Ave; (206) 682-4646; www.undergroundtour.com

Smith Tower: 506 2nd Ave; adm for observation deck; www.smithtower.com

King Street Station: 303 S Jackson St; open 24 hours daily

Klondike Gold Rush National Historical Park: 319 2nd Ave S; (206) 220-4240; open winter: 10am–5pm Tue–Sun, summer: 9am–5pm daily; www.nps.gov

Waterfall Garden Park: 219 2nd Ave South; (206) 624-6096; open 8am–3:45pm Sat & Sun

MERCHANTS CA

7 Smith Tower
Built in 1914 by typewriter tycoon L. C. Smith, this skyscraper **(left)**, at 38 stories, was once the tallest edifice *(see p39)* west of New York. Renovated in 2015, it has an observation deck with a bar and sweeping views.

8 King Street Station
The upper floors of this beautifully restored train station have been transformed into an art gallery and space for cultural events.

NISQUALLY EARTHQUAKE

In February 2001, the entire Puget Sound region experienced a 40-second earthquake *(see p37)*, measuring 6.8 on the Richter scale. Several otherwise sturdy and fireproof brick-and-mortar constructions from post-1889 were damaged.

Pioneer Square

10 Klondike Gold Rush National Historical Park
A versatile display of exhibits, films, and photographs charts Seattle's role as the closest US city to the Alaskan gold rush *(see p36)*, and its role as a crucial supply post for claim-stakers.

6 Bill Speidel's Underground Tour
Deliberately unusual in name and nature, this tour presents a remarkable look at the area's underground history. The Great Fire, tidal patterns, and poor sewage design forced citizens to convert second stories into first, shown through this subterranean 75-minute walk starting from the Pioneer Building *(see p39)*.

9 Waterfall Garden Park
This tiny private park is an oasis in the middle of the city. Relax and meditate by its 22-ft (7-m) artificial waterfall **(below)**.

TOP 10 ⭐ Chinatown-International District

Settled by Asian Americans in the late 19th century, the bustling Chinatown-International District still serves as the cultural hub for the city's Chinese, Japanese, Filipino, Vietnamese, Korean, and Laotian residents. The district's name was established by a 1999 city ordinance and today the area includes three distinct neighborhoods — Chinatown, Japantown, and Little Saigon.

1 Wing Luke Museum
The vision of civic leader Wing Luke, who died in a plane crash in 1965, this interesting museum **(below)** explores the culture, history, and influence of Asian Pacific Americans through a series of permanent and visiting exhibitions (see p41).

2 Tsue Chong Co. Inc.
This factory store has been making delicious noodles for over 100 years. They also produce fortune cookies in a variety of flavors.

3 Dim Sum
Seattleites are famously serious about their food, and the Chinatown-International District is known for these steamed Chinese delicacies. The best places can be found around S King St and S Jackson St, and are cheap and cheerful.

4 Seattle Best Tea
Tea finds its rightful place in a city overrun by coffee shops. Joe Hsu's small, modern shop **(left)** is the place to go to sample from a large range of teas. Prices range from $25 to $700 per pound.

5 Panama Hotel Tea & Coffee House
This historic building, adjacent to the Panama Hotel (see p119), was once a bathhouse. Now it is a bed and breakfast with a tea and coffee-house open to the public.

6 Uwajimaya
Established in 1928, this is the largest Asian grocery and specialty store in the Pacific Northwest. It sells sauces, meats, seafood, home decor, gifts, and art supplies, and has a deli and food court.

Previous pages Alki Point Lighthouse, seen from Alki Beach Park

8 Union Station

Opened in 1911, this Beaux Arts-style former train station (left) boasts a black-and-white mosaic floor and a 55-ft (16-m) vaulted ceiling that supports hundreds of lights. It was sensationally remodeled in 2000, and is now popular as an events venue.

CHINESE LUNAR NEW YEAR

A traditional celebration in Chinese communities worldwide, Seattle's version takes place inside the historic Union Station. Kung Fu lion dances, music, and firework displays make for a festive day.

9 T-Mobile Park and CenturyLink Field

Seattle's professional baseball, football, and soccer teams are based in these sports stadiums located close to each other.

Chinatown-International District

Kung Fu lion dance, Chinese Lunar New Year

7 Great Wall Shopping Mall

This 9-acre (3.6-ha) mall is home to a variety of Asian stores, including a large supermarket. It is a fair drive to the east of Sea-Tac Airport, but the sheer size and selection of these import stores is worth seeing.

10 Little Saigon

The storefronts here resemble images of 1960s-era Saigon, with large, bright signage in Vietnamese.

NEED TO KNOW

MAP L6 ▪ (206) 382-1197 ▪ www.cidbia.org

Wing Luke Museum: 719 S King St; (206) 623-5124; open 10am–5pm Tue–Sun (to 8pm on 1st Thu of month); adm; www.wingluke.org

Tsue Chong Co. Inc.: 800 S Weller St; (206) 623-0801; open 9:30am–5:30pm Mon–Fri, 10am–2pm Sat; www.tsuechong.com

Seattle Best Tea: 506 S King St; (206) 749-9855; open winter: 10:30am–8pm daily, summer: 10am–10pm daily

Uwajimaya: 600 5th Ave S; open 8am–10pm Mon–Sat, 9am–9pm Sun; www.uwajimaya.com

Great Wall Shopping Mall: 18230 E Valley Hwy, Kent; open 9am–9pm daily; www.greatwallmall.com

Union Station: 401 S Jackson St; (206) 398-5000

T-Mobile Park: 1250 1st Ave S; (206) 346-4000

CenturyLink Field: 800 Occidental Ave S; (206) 381-7555

▪ Try delicious dim sum at Jade Garden (424 7th Ave S) or Dim Sum King (617 S Jackson St).

⭐ Broadway

This is the main drag that slices across Capitol Hill, the coolest neighborhoods in Seattle, and the heart of the city's LGBTQ+ community. Affectionately called the "living room of Capitol Hill", Broadway features vintage stores, upbeat music venues, a variety of restaurants, and trendy cafés, all of which help to foster a thriving arts, music, and foodie scene. On summer nights, Broadway hums with activity and is an exciting place for people-watching, theater-going, and bar-hopping.

Unicorn 1

Serving up incredible cocktails, this bar **(right)** is part carnival arcade and part circus. Drag shows are performed on weekends and are strictly for those over 21.

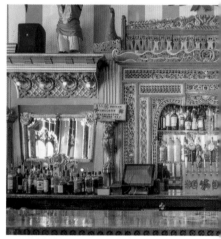

NEED TO KNOW

MAP L3–M3

Unicorn: 1118 E Pike St; (206) 325-6492; www.unicornseattle.com

Broadway Performance Hall: 1625 Broadway; (206) 325-3113; theatres.seattlecentral.edu

The Elliott Bay Book Company: 1521 10th Ave; (206) 624-6600; www.elliottbaybook.com

Dick's Drive-In: 115 Broadway Ave E; (206) 323-1300; www.ddir.com

The Vajra: 518 Broadway Ave E; (206) 323-7846; www.thevajra.com

Capitol Hill Broadway Farmers Market: Broadway Ave E and E Pine St; www.seattlefarmersmarkets.org

Cal Anderson Park: 11th between E Pine St / E Denny Way

▪ Capitol Hill hosts PrideFest in June, which celebrates Seattle's LGBTQ+ community.

Broadway Performance Hall 2

Originally Broadway High School, this stately performance hall *(see p53)* is now a part of the campus for Seattle Central College. Seattle architect Victor Steinbrueck was an instrumental figure in restoring this structure. Its repertoire includes film festivals and music and dance recitals.

The Elliott Bay Book Company 3

This destination store **(right)** offers more than 150,000 books, frequent author talks and events, and – of course – a café.

Dick's Drive-In 4

Open since 1954, this is Seattle's very own version of a fast-food hamburger joint. Alongside burgers, it also serves hand-whipped ice cream. This branch is a magnet for locals on weekend nights.

7 Dance Steps on Broadway

Sculptor Jack Mackie created an amusing series of inlaid bronze dance steps along the sidewalks of Broadway in 1982. Each one features the instructions of a dance style, such as the rumba **(left)**, the tango, and the foxtrot.

PILL HILL

This is an affectionate nickname for First Hill, an area almost indistinct from Capitol Hill along the same high ridge above downtown. It is home to most of the area's medical research facilities and hospitals.

9 Jimi Hendrix Statue

This bronze sculpture *(see p80)* of rock legend Jimi Hendrix is located by the popular Pike/Pine corridor.

Broadway

5 SIFF Cinema Egyptian

Broadway's vintage movie house *(see p53)* showcases independent films from directors on the vanguard. The Seattle International Film Festival *(see p62)* makes liberal use of the theater each year.

6 The Vajra

The name roughly translates as "Destroyer of Ignorance". This store sells a selection of Buddhist meditation supplies. Look for block-print tapestries, scented oils, and incense. It is also a popular spot for tarot-card reading.

8 Capitol Hill Broadway Farmers Market

Set up in the day time every Sunday, this market offers locally grown produce, crafts, and tasty snacks, all to the tune of friendly chatter and live music.

10 Cal Anderson Park

Named after one of Washington's openly gay legislators, the park features Lincoln Reservoir, Bobby Morris Playfield, tennis courts, a play area, and an interactive water feature **(below)**.

Lake Washington Ship Canal

TOP 10 ⭐

What began in Montlake as a tiny log flume is now a large urban waterway. In 1854, pioneer Thomas Mercer recognized the need for a passage to the ocean from Lake Union and Lake Washington, and the Ship Canal and locks were finished in 1934 by the US Army Corps of Engineers. A feat of engineering, this 8-mile (13-km) canal provides an easy passage for sailboats, kayakers, and an impressive fleet of industrial vessels heading to sea.

1 Montlake

At the base of Capitol Hill's northeastern tip, the affluent community of Montlake abuts the arboretum and the Ship Canal. Just across the canal, the university's huge Husky Stadium *(see p28)* dominates the view. The annual Opening Day Boat Parade **(above)** attracts large numbers of spectators to the canal.

2 Working Waterfront

The maritime industry prospers along the canal. Tankers lie in dry dock, boat dealers proliferate, and oil booms float about while the natural ecology struggles to survive.

3 Making the Cut

Seattle-based district engineer for the Army Corps of Engineers, Hiram M. Chittenden lobbied Congress to fund the project in 1911, and Lake Washington was leveled for boat traffic.

NEED TO KNOW
MAP B2–E2

Visitor Center: 3015 NW 54th St; open May–Sep: 10am–12:30pm & 1:30–6pm daily, Oct–Apr: 10am–12:30pm & 1:30–4pm Thu–Mon

Grounds: open 7am–9pm daily

Ballard Locks: 3015 NW 54th St; (206) 783-7059; www.ballardlocks.org

■ Those planning to go kayaking should be wary of weather changes all round the year. Strong winds can severely affect the canal's current and water conditions.

Lake Washington Ship Canal

4 Lake Union

This is an urban lake with Seattle's downtown skyline framing its southern shore **(below)**. Visit Seattle's maritime museum, the Center for Wooden Boats *(see p40)*, and Lake Union Park at the south end.

7 Bascule Bridges

These bridges operate with cantilevered sections that can be raised and lowered. Fremont and Ballard bridges are the oldest, built in 1917. The former is only 30 ft (9 m) above the waterline.

9 Urban Wildlife

Although the Ship Canal is literally and figuratively far from any wilderness, it still attracts diverse wildlife. Keep a lookout for blue heron, gulls, beaver, Canada geese, as well as migrating salmon.

5 Christmas Ships

Every December, local boaters celebrate the holiday season by venturing out during several cold evenings after decorating their boats with colorful light displays.

8 Shilshole Bay

The western end of the Ship Canal feeds into this scenic bay, home to a public marina. The waterfront boasts meeting spaces, fine seafood restaurants, and Golden Gardens park *(see p45)*.

6 Ballard Locks

Officially called the Hiram M. Chittenden Locks, these locks **(below)** link Puget Sound and Salmon Bays at Ballard. About 100,000 vessels pass through annually, as do salmon runs in the adjacent fish ladder – fully equipped with observation windows.

10 Sleepless in Seattle

The idiosyncratic floating home enclaves **(above)** of northern Lake Union and Portage Bay are visible almost exclusively by boats traveling the canal. One was a focal point in the romantic film, *Sleepless in Seattle* (1993), starring Meg Ryan and Tom Hanks.

🔟 ⭐ University of Washington

Founded in November 1861, just ten years after the creation of Washington Territory, the prestigious UW moved to its present location with 639 hilly acres (258 ha) in 1895. Supporting a student body that is as eclectic as the architectural mix on campus, the institution has garnered an international reputation. The wide-open quads, cherry blossoms in spring, and lovely views provide a relaxing counterpoint to the buzz of advanced learning.

University campus

1 Henry Art Gallery
Founded in 1927, this was the state's first public art gallery **(above)**. The Henry *(see p40)* is world renowned for its special focus on photography, as well as digital and projected media. It also has a café and a bookstore.

2 Suzzallo Library
Once known as "the soul of the University," the library is the crowning glory of the Neo-Gothic style on campus. The astounding vaulted ceiling rises 65 ft (20 m) above the second floor reading room **(below)**.

3 Husky Stadium
Located at Capitol Hill's northeastern tip, the upscale Montlake abuts the arboretum and the Ship Canal *(see pp26–7)*. Just across the canal sits the university's huge Husky Stadium, home of the UW Huskies.

4 Meany Center
The shining glory of professional performance arts on campus, the theater hosts performers of all disciplines from all over the globe. It also supports all of the school's drama, music, dance, and experimental digital media curricula.

5 Cherry Blossoms
Photographers, tourists, and painters flock to the Quad on campus during early spring to witness an annual spectacle – the Yoshino cherry trees in full bloom. These stunning trees were donated by the mayor of Tokyo in 1912, marking a friendly alliance between Japan and the United States.

6 University Book Store
The main branch of the bookstore rivals the best of the independent and larger chain book vendors for sheer selection and well-informed staff.

University of Washington

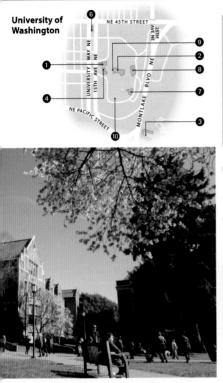

MAP E2–F2

THE AVE

The main commercial artery serving the U District is University Way NE, called "The Ave". It is lined with coffee shops, clothiers, boutique shops, bars, and restaurants serving reasonably priced food.

10 Medicinal Herb Garden

Escape for a captivating stroll through 2.5 acres (1 ha) of land **(below)** where several hundred species flourish and herbal scents abound.

NEED TO KNOW

MAP E2–F2 ■ (206) 543-2100 ■ www.washington.edu

Henry Art Gallery: NE 41st St & 15th Ave NE; open 10am–7pm Thu (to 5pm Fri–Sun); adm (free 1st Thu of month); www.henry art.org

Husky Stadium: 3800 Montlake Blvd; www.gohuskies.com

Meany Center: 4040 George Washington Lane NE; (206) 543-4880; www.meany center.org

University Book Store: 4326 University Way NE; (206) 634-3400; www.ubookstore.com

7 Paul G. Allen Center for Computer Science & Engineering

This $72-million state-of-the-art facility **(below)** was named after one of the two founders of Microsoft.

8 The Hub

The main student union building is known as "The Hub" due to its central position on campus. It is information central, as well as a venue for performers.

9 Red Square

Taking its name from the inlaid brick paving stones underfoot, the huge square lies between the Meany Center, Kane Hall, and the Suzzallo Library. It is also known for hosting impromptu midnight concerts.

Seattle Art Museum

Founded as a local fine arts society in 1906, the Seattle Art Museum (SAM) has grown into a world-class visual arts center with sculptures, paintings, carvings, and other treasures. The modern, limestone-clad building that houses the SAM has gone through several expansions to accommodate this ever-growing collection of fine art. Its exterior is guarded by the 48-ft (15-m) tall *Hammering Man* by American sculptor Jonathan Borofsky – a black steel installation that silently hammers away for 20 hours a day, commemorating the everyday worker.

1 Middle Fork
Suspended above the entrance is a stunning sculpture by local artist John Grade. It was created from a full plaster cast of a living – and unharmed – 150-year old western hemlock tree found in the Cascade Mountains. The 105-ft- (32-m-) long sculpture was then pieced together with thousands of bits of reclaimed cedar.

Iconic sculpture of the Hammering Man by Borofsky

2 African Art
Level four of the museum displays unique West African sculptures **(above)** that date back as far as the 15th-century. Highlights include a century-old wooden headdress from Nigeria, and a brass plaque from the 16th-century detailing the life of a soldier in the Kingdom of Benin.

3 Ancient Mediterranean Art
Admire this remarkable collection of artifacts and art from the Ancient Mediterranean, including ancient Egyptian relics. Among the many historic treasures on display, there are exhibits such as a delicate glass cosmetic bottle, several 2,000-year-old Greek silver coins, a fine 3rd-century Roman mosaic piece, and much more.

4 Modern and Contemporary Art
The works of several iconic abstract artists are featured in this gallery, including Jackson Pollock's painting *Sea Change*, and Howard Kottler's modern ceramic sculpture *Kottler Posing as a Cubist*, which is glazed with a gold finish. Visitors can also find Katharina Fritsch's whimsical *Mann und Maus*, an installation of a giant mouse sitting on the chest of a sleeping man.

5 American Art

Notable American artists are featured in this exhibit. There are works depicting a range of styles, such as Modernism, Abstract, Realism, and Post-Impressionism. Among the highlights are John Covert's sparingly abstract *The Temptation of St. Anthony #2*.

6 Islamic Art

This gallery showcases fine art connected to Middle Eastern Islamic culture **(below)**. Highlights include a lovely Turkish tile from the 16th-century.

7 Native Art of the Americas

Works by both US Native American and Canadian First Nations artists are displayed in this gallery. Exhibits include striking masks from the 1940s by Kwakwaka'wakw artists and a tiny, intricately carved Haida chest **(above)** from the 1880s.

8 Australian Art

An intimate gallery space showcasing a rotating exhibit of works by the Aboriginal people from Australia. It holds the painting *Leaves* by the artist Gloria Petyarre of the Anmatyerr people. This highly detailed and monochromatic piece is a part of her series of batik-style works.

9 European Art

Masterful works can be viewed in this gallery including the paintings *Winter Landscape on the Banks of the Seine* by French artist Henri Matisse and Santi Di Tito's classical *Portrait of a Young Woman*.

THE ODALISQUE

In 1999, the Seattle Art Museum returned a highly valuable Henri Matisse painting, *Odalisque*, to its rightful owners. The piece was stolen by the Nazis during World War II. It was the first time in history that a private individual retrieved stolen art from an American museum. From then onwards, SAM ensures to triple-check its collection's provenance.

10 Japanese Teahouse

Experience and learn about *chado*, the precise art of tea culture from Japan, which is hosted inside a traditional teahouse. Designed and built in Japan, the teahouse was reassembled in the museum by Japanese carpenters. Guests are offered green tea and sweets.

NEED TO KNOW

MAP J4 ■ 1300 1st Ave ■ (206) 654-3100 ■ www.seattleartmuseum.org

Open 10am–5pm Wed–Sun

Adm adults $19.99; seniors (65 and above) $17.99; students (with ID) & teens (15–18) $12.99; children (14 and under) free; free adm on first Thu

■ The main galleries of the museum can be found on the third and fourth floors. The third floor has the Modern and Contemporary Art, American Art, and Native Art of the Americas, and other galleries. The fourth floor holds galleries on European Art, African Art, Ancient Mediterranean, and Islamic Art, alongside a space for special exhibitions. On the first floor there is a shop and a restaurant, and on the second is the visitor information desk, ticketing and coat check.

TOP10 ⭐ Discovery Park

Spanning the northwestern edge of the Magnolia headland north of Elliott Bay, Discovery Park is Seattle's largest and most varied in-city escape. It occupies a large section of the historic Fort Lawton site, a former post of the United States Army. Covering an expanse of 534 acres (216 ha) and home to more than 250 species of fauna, the park consists of densely wooded rainforests crisscrossed with trails, high bluffs of eroding sand at the edge of a huge meadow, and stunning driftwood-laden beaches on Puget Sound.

NEED TO KNOW

MAP A2 ▪ (206) 684-4075 ▪ www. seattle.gov/parks

Open 4am–11:30pm daily

Visitors' Center: 3801 Discovery Park Blvd; (206) 386-4236; open 8:30am–5pm Tue–Sun

Daybreak Star Indian Cultural Center: (206) 285-4425; www.united indians.org

▪ The Visitor Center has clean restrooms.

▪ There aren't any concessions in the park, so bring a picnic lunch.

① Eagle-Watching

Occasionally, bald eagles nest in the highest treetops in Discovery Park, home to more than 270 species of birds and other wildlife. You may find park volunteers surrounded by eager bird-watchers with binoculars. Chances are they have sighted a nest.

② Daybreak Star Indian Cultural Center

The United Indians of All Tribes Foundation, operates this cultural center, home to an interesting collection of Indigenous art. There is also an arts and crafts gallery, traditional salmon bakes, and an annual summer Pow Wow celebration featuring dancers and musicians in the park.

Discovery Park

4 Playground

For an outing with children, head to the playground **(left)** behind park head-quarters at the east entrance. Located among tall trees, the playground has two multi-level climbing structures, a zip line, and multiple accessible features for all abilities.

5 Military Residences

The park is dotted with former army base housing, listed on the National Register of Historic Places. Most are off-limits and under redevelopment, but can be observed near the former parade grounds.

6 Beach Walks at Low Tide

Seattleites escaping the city come to walk along the waterfront parks around the Sound. The beach **(left)** at Discovery Park is a preferred spot for those in the know.

3 West Point Treatment Plant

A reminder of the city outside, this facility is so exquisitely landscaped as to be almost invisible from hiking trails. This ultramodern wastewater treatment plant is about as environmentally conscious as today's technology allows.

7 West Point Lighthouse

As picturesque as can be, the lighthouse **(below)** shines light through the rolling fog from its high perch on a narrow spit of land jutting out into the water. Its automated sentinel is not open for touring, but visitors can stroll around it.

SHARING THE LAND

Land use at Discovery Park represents the harmonious balance between urban develop-ment and conservation. In 1970, activist Bernie Whitebear staged an occupation of the still-active US military base, in part to establish a cultural land founda-tion for urban Indians. After battling for three months, Whitebear's group acquired a 99-year parkland lease.

8 Bluff Trail

The trail **(below)** leads from the South Gate along a meadow's edge to the overlook, with views of Puget Sound and the Olympic Mountains.

9 Loop Trail

Stroll along this trail through the varied terrain of Discovery Park. Explore the easy route to find overgrown rainforest ravines, flowering mead-owlands, creeks, sand dunes, thickets, and brambles galore.

10 Go Fly a Kite

The hilly field between the main bluffs and a radar ball behind barbed wire makes for some of the best kite fly-ing around, as the sea updrafts seem constant.

The Top 10 of Everything

Detail of Frank Gehry's visionary
exterior of the Museum of Pop Culture

TOP 10 Moments in History

Illustration depicting 18th-century lumber merchants on Puget Sound

1 Native American Roots

Archaeological records date the first inhabitants of the Seattle region to 11,000–12,000 years ago. Early settlers included the Nisqually, Suquamish, Duwamish, Snoqualmie, and Muckleshoot Tribes.

2 Denny Party

In 1851, Chief Sealth of the Duwamish Tribe met Arthur A. Denny and his group of European settlers at West Seattle's Alki Point (see p104). Seattle's founding dates from this meeting. Subsequently, Denny served as a delegate to the Monticello convention, which gave rise to the states of Oregon and Washington.

Seattle Monument on Alki Beach

3 Northern Pacific Railroad

Seattle's neighboring city, Tacoma, was the original terminus of 1873's Northern Pacific Railroad, linking the region to the rest of the country. By 1893, another transcontinental railroad, the Great Northern Railway, extended into Seattle, eventually supplanting Tacoma as the Puget Sound region's main rail depot.

4 Lumber Mills

When timber baron Frederick Weyerhaeuser purchased nearly 1,550 sq miles (4,000 sq km) of railroad land in 1900, Seattle's mushrooming logging industry turned a corner for even more rapid growth and exploitation of natural resources. Until then, entrepreneurs such as Henry Yesler ruled the wharf, and erected the pioneer town out of lumber from ancient old-growth forests.

5 Great Fire of 1889

Natural resources created a boomtown whose rapid growth drew more than 1,000 new residents every month. Seattleites learned the fragility of wooden structures in 1889, after a catastrophic fire destroyed much of the downtown area.

6 Klondike Gold Rush

The Alaska Gold Rush (see p19) officially kicked off in 1897 after a gold-filled steamship docked at Seattle's waterfront. As the last stop for prospectors and suppliers bound for the gold fields, the city prospered.

7 Boeing's Beginnings

Recognizing the need for airplanes as the US entered World War I in 1917, William E. Boeing hired pilot Herb Munter to design a seaplane for the Navy. Boeing is now the world's largest aerospace company, after Airbus.

8 Rise of Microsoft

In 1975, Harvard dropout Bill Gates and his high-school friend Paul Allen founded Microsoft from the Seattle suburb of Redmond. The rise of Microsoft attracted the best talent and many new tech start-ups to the city, making it the country's epicenter of tech development. Today, Microsoft's Seattle neighbors include tech giants such as Google, Amazon, and Expedia.

Microsoft's Bill Gates and Paul Allen

9 Nisqually Earthquake

Seattle suffered from a major magnitude-6.8 earthquake on the morning of February 28, 2001 (see p19). Workers escaped their offices, if they could, to see the earth rolling, pavements cracking, and cars violently swaying. The region suffered more than $1 billion in damages.

10 Great Wheel Opens

In 2012, the Seattle Great Wheel opened on Pier 57 overlooking Puget Sound, adding a major attraction to the waterfront and bringing new life to the area. The 175-ft- (53-m-) tall Ferris wheel is open daily.

TOP 10 FAMOUS SEATTLEITES

Kung fu legend Bruce Lee

1 Chief Sealth (1786–1866)
Seattle draws its name from the Suquamish and Duwamish leader.

2 John W. Nordstrom (1871–1963)
Originally shoe sellers, the Nordstrom family empire is now a national chain of upscale department stores.

3 Nellie Centennial Cornish (1876–1956)
A great pioneer of the Seattle art scene, she founded the Cornish College of the Arts in 1914.

4 Cecile Anne Hansen (b. 1934)
The chairwoman of the Duwamish Tribe and descendant of Chief Sealth is an advocate for the recognition of Seattle's first people.

5 Bruce Lee (1940–1973)
This kung fu legend and movie star lived in Seattle and is buried here.

6 Jimi Hendrix (1942–1970)
A self-taught guitarist and legend, Hendrix continues to influence today's music with his original compositions.

7 Nancy Pearl (b. 1945)
The celebrity librarian was author of *Book Lust*, and is an ambassador for a city full of readers.

8 Gary Locke (b. 1950)
The first Chinese-American governor in US history, Locke also served as Secretary of Commerce and the US Ambassador to China.

9 Paul Allen (1953-2018)
Co-founder of Microsoft and an important philanthropist.

10 Jeff Bezos (b. 1964)
This multi-billionaire founded giant web retailer Amazon in 1995, and is now the world's richest man.

🔟 Architectural Highlights

Colored sheet-metal exterior of the Museum of Pop Culture

1 Museum of Pop Culture
Frank Gehry, a world-renowned Post Modern architect, designed this technicolor edifice (see pp14–15). It resembles a smashed guitar, in provocative homage to Seattle-born Jimi Hendrix's famed finales. The brainchild of Microsoft co-founder Paul Allen, it emphasizes Seattle's role in the artistic and musical movement.

2 Central Library
Award-winning Dutch architect Rem Koolhaas designed this $196 million insulated glass-and-steel building (see p72) to replace Seattle's vintage 1960 Central Library. The unusual oblique structure and glass flooring have been controversial, but its defenders insist that, once inside, people will love it.

3 Columbia Center
This imposing 76-story skyscraper (see p73) rises higher than any other structure in Seattle. Completed in 1985, from a design by Chester Lindsey Architects, it is one of the tallest buildings on the West Coast. Three of the 48 elevators bring visitors to the posh private club at the top. There is also an observation deck on the 73rd floor that offers stunning panoramic views across Elliott Bay, the Olympic Peninsula, Mount Rainier, and beyond to the Cascade Mountains.

4 The Spheres
MAP J3 ■ 2111 7th Ave ■ Open 10am–6pm 1st & 3rd Sat of month ■ www.seattlespheres.com
Online retail giant Amazon conceived this complex as a greenhouse-like social center. The three conjoined globes resemble water molecules and the scaffolding is visible through the greenish glass skin. Entry and tours require advance booking.

5 Space Needle
Seattle's modern architectural identity began with the Space Needle (see p15), designed by architect firm John Graham & Company, for the 1962 World's Fair. The three pairs of beams supporting the spire lie buried 30 ft (8 m) underground, and have secured the 605-ft (185-m) Needle during several earthquakes and gale-force windstorms.

Iconic Space Needle

6 Rainier Tower
MAP K4 ▪ 1301 5th Ave

Designed by renowned architect Minoru Yamasaki in 1977, this unique 41-story structure resembles an upside-down skyscraper, as its main tower rises from a relatively narrow 11-story pedestal. Rainier Square, an upscale underground mall, is located beneath the tower.

7 Smith Tower

Typewriter tycoon L. C. Smith erected Seattle's first skyscraper (see pp18–19) in 1914. The white terra-cotta building has brass hand-operated elevators that take visitors to a bar at the 35th level, with its antique carvings, inlaid porcelain ceiling, and an observation deck.

8 Seattle Tower
MAP K4 ▪ 1218 3rd Ave

This charming Art Deco building was designed by architects Albertson, Wilson & Richardson in 1929. The facade's tan brick and many shades of granite set this tower apart from its steel-and-glass neighbors. Vertical accents make its 27 stories appear even taller, and the lobby's ornate bronze and marble detail is capped by a decorative ceiling bas-relief.

9 Seattle Center Monorail

One of the city's favorite attractions is taking an exciting two-minute ride on the monorail (see p15) designed by Alweg Rapid Transit Systems. Each year, 1.5 million passengers board its original 1962 cars to get a taste of what designers imagined at the time would be the mass transit model of the future. The monorail connects the Seattle Center with the downtown area, and departures take place every ten minutes from the Westlake Center Station (5th & Pine Sts) and the Seattle Center.

Pioneer Building facade

10 Pioneer Building
MAP K5 ▪ 608 1st Ave

Built of red brick and glazed terra-cotta, this 1892 building was designed by Elmer H. Fisher. It was the city's tallest building until 1904, and boasts a National Historic Landmark status. During the Gold Rush years (see p36), 48 mining outfits maintained offices here, and it became headquarters for a speakeasy during Prohibition. Bill Speidel's Underground Tour (see pp18–19) starts here.

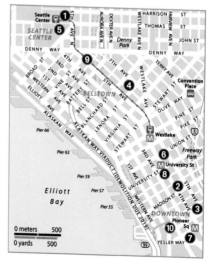

TOP 10 Museums

1 Henry Art Gallery

This modern art museum *(see pp28–9)* at UW presents work by cutting-edge artists. It also offers numerous imaginative programs and exhibits, and promotes experimental art by encouraging dialogue on contemporary culture and aesthetics.

Temporary exhibit, Henry Art Gallery

2 Seattle Asian Art Museum

MAP E4 ■ 1400 E Prospect St ■ (206) 654-3100 ■ Open 10am–5pm Fri–Sun ■ www.seattleart museum.org

The historic Art-Moderne structure in Volunteer Park was built in 1933. It now houses Seattle Art Museum's Asian art collection.

3 Frye Art Museum

MAP L4 ■ 704 Terry Ave ■ (206) 622-9250 ■ Open 11am–5pm Wed–Sun ■ www. fryemuseum.org

Wealthy industrialists Emma and Charles Frye's collection of 19th- to 20th-century representational art is on view at this elegant gallery.

Exhibits include works by American masters such as Mary Cassatt, John Singer Sargent, and Andrew Wyeth.

4 Chihuly Garden and Glass

Famous glass sculptor Dale Chihuly's striking glass artworks are displayed at the Seattle Center *(see p14)*. Chihuly is known to have led the development of glass as a fine art. Today, his work is included in more than 200 major museums around the world. The Seattle Center features eight galleries, a centerpiece glass house, a colorful installation in the garden, and a theater that presents videos of Chihuly blowing glass at the hotshop.

5 Center for Wooden Boats

MAP K1 ■ 1010 Valley St ■ (206) 382-2628 ■ Open 10am–6pm Tue–Sun ■ www.cwb.org

CWB has over 100 small vessels and offers classes in maritime activities and crafts. During its annual festival in July, relic sloops and tugs can be toured. For an in-city adventure, try sailing one of the historic boats.

6 Seattle Art Museum

The tall, black metal *Hammering Man* by Jonathan Borofsky stands outside Seattle's largest art museum *(see pp30–31)*. SAM's permanent collection includes Asian, European, African, and Native American works.

European Gallery, Seattle Art Museum

Museum of History & Industry exhibit

(7) Museum of History & Industry

MAP K1 ▪ 860 Terry Ave N ▪ (206) 324-1126 ▪ Open 10am–5pm daily (to 8pm Thu) ▪ Adm (free 1st Thu of month) ▪ www.mohai.org

Located in Lake Union Park, this is a gem for anyone interested in the region's work and workforce over the last 150 years. Key features of this museum include photographs and a rich library of oral histories.

(8) Museum of Flight

MAP P2 ▪ 9404 E Marginal Way S ▪ (206) 764-5700 ▪ Open 10am–5pm daily (to 9pm 1st Thu of month) ▪ Adm (free 1st Thu of month) ▪ www.museumofflight.org

Walk through a model of the Space Shuttle, tour the first Air Force One, designed for President Kennedy, climb into the cockpit of a SR-71 Blackbird or F/A-18 Hornet jet, or step aboard Concorde (see p50).

(9) Northwest African American Museum

MAP F6 ▪ 2300 S Massachusetts St ▪ (206) 518-6000 ▪ Open 11am–5pm Wed–Sun (to 7pm Thu) ▪ Adm (free 1st Thu of month) ▪ www.naamnw.org

Visitors can trace the history and traditions of African-Americans in the Pacific Northwest at this museum, which also hosts regular events.

(10) Wing Luke Museum

Named after a civic leader who lobbied for Asian-American rights, this museum (see p22) fulfills Wing's dream to showcase the culture and history of Asian immigrants.

TOP 10 NORTHWEST ARTISTS

1 Mark Tobey (1890–1976)
A 1953 *Life* magazine featured Tobey as one of the four "Mystic Painters of the Pacific Northwest." He was a major influence on Jackson Pollock.

2 Kenneth Callahan (1905–1986)
Another artist in the aforementioned *Life* feature, Callahan was once a curator at Seattle Art Museum.

3 Paul Horiuchi (1906–1999)
Japan-born Horiuchi used heavily textured, Abstract Expressionist collage painting utilizing Zen philosophy to create his mysterious works.

4 George Tsutakawa (1910–1997)
He gained international fame as a painter, sculptor, and fountain-maker.

5 Morris Graves (1910–2001)
The work of this Northwest painter continues to inspire Seattle artists.

6 Jacob Lawrence (1917–2000)
Lawrence established a national reputation as a painter and activist.

7 Fay Jones (b. 1936)
The monumental painter behind the Pop Art Westlake tunnel mural, Jones's work can be seen at SAM.

8 Dale Chihuly (b. 1941)
Chihuly's handblown decorative glass art has popularized the medium.

9 Barbara Earl Thomas (b. 1948)
The first director of the Northwest African American Museum is a recipient of the local "Genius" award.

10 Debora Moore (b. 1960)
Once a member of Dale Chihuly's team, this glass artist is best-known for her monumental glass orchids.

Portrait of Jacob Lawrence

TOP 10 The Eastside

Seattle's two floating bridges

 Floating Bridges
MAP P2

Lake Washington's famous floating bridges, the Interstate 90 and the State Route 520 toll bridge, connect Seattle with the suburb of Bellevue and the Eastside. The highways' middle portions rest on the water's surface above air-filled pontoons that support tons of traffic as well as concrete. Occasional windstorms push waves of water onto the road, creating back ups for commuters.

2 Kirkland
MAP P2

Once a small rural town across Lake Washington, Kirkland has grown into a sprawling suburb with the resident Microsoft executives and managers giving it a reputation for expensive real estate. It is also known for its charming waterfront that offers great shopping and dining options along with fantastic beaches that provide ample views of Seattle and the Olympic Mountains beyond.

 Microsoft Visitor Center
MAP P2 ■ 15010 NE 36th St, Redmond ■ (425) 703-6214 ■ Opening hours vary; call ahead

Learn more about the history, products, and vision of the software giant at this high-tech visitor center located on the Redmond campus.

Big screens, interactive exhibits, and a timeline bring the culture of Microsoft to life. Visitors can explore the latest developments in gaming technology, mobile devices, and more.

4 Luther Burbank Park
MAP P2 ■ 2040 84th Ave SE, Mercer Island ■ Open 6am–10pm daily

A small affluent community just off Interstate 90, Mercer Island is known for its lovely waterfront park. Located on the northeastern tip of the island, it offers boaters and visitors several notable attractions, including tennis courts, a playground, and trails that lead to a swimming area and fishing dock. On Sunday afternoons in the summer, the park hosts interesting theater productions and free concerts in its amphitheater.

5 The Gates' Estate
MAP P2 ■ 1835 73rd Ave NE, Medina

So many people wonder how and where one of the world's richest men lives. Microsoft's founder, Bill Gates, built his estate on Lake Washington's eastern shore, installing the latest technological advancements in modern living such as high-end security systems, customized touch and voice controls, and luxurious entertainment facilities. The estate is not open to the public, but it is visible from the water, and touring boats occasionally cruise within sight from a considerable distance.

Seattle's skyline, viewed from Old Bellevue

⑥ Eastside Wineries

Chateau Ste. Michelle: MAP P2; 14111 NE 145th St, Woodinville; (425) 488-1133; www.ste-michelle.com

Chateau Ste. Michelle is Washington state's oldest winery. The 87-acre (35-ha) wooded estate in Woodinville, 15 miles (24 km) north of Seattle, hosts tours and well-attended summer concerts. It is one of several outfits taking advantage of a climate that favors excellent grape varieties. Other wine producers include Columbia Crest, DeLille Cellars, the Betz Family Winery, and Finn Hill Winery.

⑦ Mercer Slough Nature Park

MAP P2 ■ 2102 Bellevue Way SE, Bellevue ■ Open dawn–dusk daily

This expansive park, built on the grounds of the largest remaining wetland on Lake Washington, has a long network of trails and esplanades. Bird-watchers flock to the Slough to view the hundreds of bird species. Other kinds of wildlife here include coyote, beaver, and muskrat. Activities comprise canoeing and kayaking, guided nature walks and pick-your-own blueberries during summer.

⑧ Old Bellevue

MAP P2

Bellevue is a classic suburb and one of the state's largest cities. But there is an area that harks back to its former life as a small town. Head to Old Bellevue and its charming, restored Main Street for the antidote to freeway interchanges and big box stores, especially if you like buying antiques.

⑨ Marymoor Park

MAP P2 ■ 6046 W Lake Sammamish Pkwy NE, Redmond ■ Open 8am–dusk daily

The county's most popular park boasts soccer and baseball fields, a velodrome, and a dog-training field, where dogs are free to roam off the leash. Park trails connect with the Sammamish River Trail, a bike route that leads to wineries in Woodinville.

⑩ The Bellevue Collection

MAP P2 ■ 575 Bellevue Sq ■ (425) 646-3660 ■ www.bellevue collection.com

These three indoor shopping malls are connected by glass bridges and contain dozens of restaurants as well as more than 200 shops, many of them upscale boutiques. There is a cinema, an arcade room, and a kids play area. Take express bus (550) from downtown Seattle to get here.

🔟 Urban Retreats

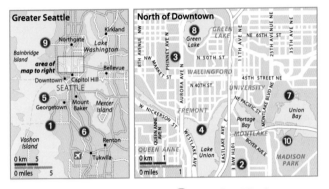

1 Lincoln Park

MAP P3 ▪ 8011 Fauntleroy Way SW ▪ (206) 684-4075

Located on the road to West Seattle's Fauntleroy Ferry Terminal (see p104), this spot is ideal for those looking for hilly trails, picnics by the water, or a dip in the Colman Pool (see p46).

Volunteer Park Conservatory

2 Volunteer Park

MAP E4 ▪ 1247 15th Ave E ▪ (206) 684-4075

Between 1904 and 1909, the Olmsted Brothers transformed these 45 acres (18 ha) of hilltop into a rustic grass meadow with a fantastic view. The park now houses the Seattle Asian Art Museum (see p40), the Volunteer Park Conservatory, and an observation tower (see p80).

3 Woodland Park Rose Garden

MAP D1 ▪ Intersection of N 50th St & Fremont Ave N ▪ (206) 548-2500

Visitors to the Woodland Park Zoo (see p97) often stumble across this gated area near one of the zoo entrances. About 3,000 individual plants and 200 varieties of rose turn this little corner of Seattle into a technicolor dream.

4 Gas Works Park

MAP D3 ▪ 2101 N Northlake Way ▪ (206) 684-4075

Set up in 1906 as a gasification plant to light the streets of Seattle, this is the first industrial site in the world to be re-created into a public park. Much of the machinery here either remains on exhibit, or sits rusting behind security fences. Among the attractions here is a high kite hill with a sundial created by artists Chuck Greening and Kim Lazare.

5 Schmitz Preserve Park

MAP A5 ▪ 5551 SW Admiral Way ▪ (206) 684-4075

The scant remains of the temperate rainforest old growth trees hint at what Seattle must have resembled before European settlement. Schmitz is a deep, wide, wooded ravine surrounded by residential streets, but street noises disappear among the magnificent trees and native plants.

6 Kubota Garden

MAP P3 ▪ 9817 55th Ave S
▪ (206) 725-5060 ▪ www.kubota
garden.org

Discover traditional Japanese landscaping in a residential neighborhood in South Seattle. With native plants, koi ponds, rock and formal bridges, a waterfall, and splendid views, this garden is a real delight, especially in spring for the blossoms, and in fall for the colors of the leaves. It is free to visit and rarely crowded.

7 Center for Urban Horticulture

MAP F2 ▪ 3501 NE 41st St ▪ (206) 543-8616 ▪ www.botanicgardens.uw.edu

The CUH was established in 1984 by the University of Washington (see pp28–9) in order to exert more control and achieve sounder management of the arboretum. It features a herb garden, a library, pretty meadows, and weekly master-gardener meetings.

8 Green Lake

MAP D1 ▪ 7201 E Green Lake Dr N ▪ (206) 684-4075

The well-worn paths in this lake's sylvan setting take visitors around the placid water in a quiet neighborhood. Gently rippling with the wind or mirror-smooth, Green Lake's mesmerizing surface invokes a sense of peace and calm. It is usually packed on weekends, especially in summer, when people flock to the grassy areas to sunbathe by the lake.

9 Golden Gardens

In Ballard's far northwestern edge along Puget Sound, the wide sandy beaches of Golden Gardens (see p98) take on the characteristics of a cherished vacation spot. The Olympic Mountains stand to their west, a marina lies adjacent, and Lake Washington Ship Canal is nearby, so pleasure crafts are always in view. There are wetlands, a wooded area, a stream, and a trail.

The waterfront Golden Gardens

10 Washington Park Arboretum and Japanese Garden

MAP F3 ▪ 2300 Arboretum Dr E ▪ Japanese Garden: 1075 Lake Washington Blvd E; adm

This beautiful arboretum (see p60) features a staggering 230 acres (93 ha) of carefully cultivated landscapes and rare tree species. The gardens were built in 1960 to plans by Japanese designer Juki Iida. These include a traditional sculpture, ponds, and a teahouse.

Washington Park Japanese Garden

TOP 10 Outdoor Activities

1 Colman Pool
MAP P2 ▪ 8603 Fauntleroy Way SW ▪ (206) 684-7494 ▪ Open late May–Aug ▪ Adm

An alternative to the cold Puget Sound is the beachside Colman Pool in Lincoln Park *(see p44)*. It uses heated and filtered saltwater from the Sound, which it overlooks.

Outdoor Colman Pool

2 Kayaking
With its Ship Canal links to Lake Washington and Shilshole, Lake Union is ideal for kayaking. The currents are easy to negotiate when there is no wind. Adventurous river-runners can opt for challenging whitewater courses closer to the mountains. To explore marine life in Puget Sound, try Alki Kayak Tours *(see pp114–15)*.

3 Snowshoe Treks
National Park Service: MAP P6; www.nps.gov

A popular winter sport, snowshoeing is an ancient method of walking on or through the snow. The National

Park Service and local outfitters offer ranger-guided walks. Beginners should start with an experienced professional guide to lead the outing.

4 Climbing Rock Walls
REI: MAP K2; 222 Yale Ave N; www.rei.com ▪ Stone Gardens: MAP B1; 2839 NW Market St; www.stonegardens.com

One of the most popular spots for indoor rock climbing is Recreational Equipment Incorporated (REI), which has a huge practice wall in its flagship store. Schurman Rock at Camp Long *(see p103)* offers outdoor climbing for free for those with gear. Stone Gardens offer classes and practice walls for members and walk-ins.

5 Burke-Gilman Trail
The legacy of two of Seattle's earliest railroad men, Judge Thomas Burke and Daniel Gilman, this disused railroad is a paved trail *(see p93)* that stretches 27 miles (43 km) from Ballard to Lake Washington. Cyclists and pedestrians can enjoy key sights such as Gas Works Park *(see p44)* and Magnuson Park at Sand Point.

6 Skiing and Snowboarding
Crystal Mountain Resort: MAP P6; 33914 Crystal Mountain Blvd, Enumclaw; www.crystalmountainresort.com

Seattleites anxiously await the first snowfall that carpets the Cascades. Crystal Mountain, Snoqualmie Pass, Alpental, and Stevens Pass attract several skilled skiers, and boarders.

Snow-covered Crystal Mountain

Scuba diving in Puget Sound

7 Scuba Diving

Seattle Dive Tours: MAP B5; 2653 SW Yancy St; www.seattledivetours.com

Discover undersea creatures such as wolf eels, octopuses, sea stars, and urchins in the Puget Sound estuary. Divers can embark solo or with chartered excursions to take advantage of a coastline that is free of dangerous currents from Pacific Ocean storms.

8 Windsurfing

Northwest Wind & Surf: (425) 610-7569

For one of the country's windsurfing meccas, head to Hood River, Oregon, in the Columbia River Gorge. Seattle has two prime spots – along the west shores of Lake Washington, between Magnuson Beach and Seward Park; and at Golden Gardens Park, where Shilshole Bay meets Puget Sound.

9 Paddle Boarding

Urban Surf: MAP D3; 2100 N Northlake Way; www.urbansurf.com

The warmer, protected waters of Lake Union are a perfect place to try this popular watersport. Rental equipment, lessons, and tours are available through Urban Surf.

10 Tolt-MacDonald Park & Campground

MAP Q2 = 31020 NE 40th St, Carnation

Many in-city parks have decent single tracks for casual mountain biking. But intermediate-level cyclists seeking a challenge in a great riverside setting should head 28 miles (45 km) east across Lake Washington to Carnation, in the Snoqualmie River valley.

TOP 10 PLACES TO RENT GEAR

1 Recreational Equipment Incorporated (REI)
This superb rock climbing spot is a mecca for outdoor recreation lovers.

2 Outdoor Research
MAP D6 = 2203 1st Ave S = www.outdoorresearch.com
A Seattle-based outlet that specializes in all-weather outdoor gear.

3 Feathered Friends
MAP K2 = 263 Yale Ave N = (206) 292-2210
This store offers a great selection of camping gear for the keen climber.

4 Agua Verde Café & Paddle Club
MAP E2 = 1307 NE Boat St = (206) 545-8570
Rent a kayak or dine on Mexican food.

5 Moss Bay Rowing & Kayaking Center
MAP K1 = 1001 Fairview Ave N = (206) 682-2031
Offers a variety of kayaks and rowboats.

6 Gregg's Greenlake Cycles
MAP E1 = 7007 Woodlawn Ave NE = (206) 523-1822
Road bikes are available for hire here.

7 Greenlake Boat Rentals
MAP E1 = 7351 East Green Lake Dr N = (206) 527-0171
Offers stand up paddle boats for rent.

8 Windworks Sailing Center
MAP A1 = 7001 Seaview Ave NW = (206) 784-9386
Rent bareboats or take sailing lessons.

9 Northwest Outdoor Center
MAP D3 = 2100 Westlake Ave N = (206) 281-9694
Rent kayaks or paddle along the Canal.

10 Center for Wooden Boats
A museum (see p40) that doubles up as a boat rental outlet.

Center for Wooden Boats

 **Off the Beaten Path**

1 Jack Block Park

MAP B5 ▪ 2130 Harbor Ave SW ▪ (206) 787-3000 ▪ Open dawn–dusk

This park offers possibly the best view in Seattle. There is a pier, a small beach, and an overlook towards the city. It is well signposted but most miss it on their way to Alki Beach.

Volunteer Park Water Tower

2 Volunteer Park Water Tower

Those who walk up 107 spiral steps of the Volunteer Park Water Tower *(see p80)* will be rewarded with a 360-degree view over the city. Between the tower windows, there are exhibits on Seattle's parks and their landscape architect, Frederick Law Olmstead.

3 SPARK Museum of Electrical Invention

MAP P4 ▪ 1312 Bay St, Bellingham ▪ (360) 738-3886 ▪ Open 11am–5pm Wed–Sun ▪ Adm ▪ www.spark museum.org

Take a drive north to Bellingham to dive into the history of electricity and radio. This delightfully nerdy collection spans objects from the 1600s and the dawn of electricity through to the golden age of radio in the 1950s.

4 West Seattle Farmers' Market

MAP A5 ▪ Alaska St & California Ave ▪ Open 10am–2pm Sun ▪ www. seattlefarmersmarkets.org/markets/ west-seattle

The city has at least a dozen weekly farmers' markets – this one has more than 70 vendors and is a good excuse to venture into an underappreciated neighborhood. It is open year-round, but is slightly smaller in winter.

5 Georgetown

MAP P2 ▪ Between S Lucile St, W Marginal Way S & Airport Way S

This changing neighborhood is home to cool diner-style breakfast joints, Georgetown Trailer Park Mall, Jules Maes Saloon, Seattle's oldest bar, art galleries and shops, Fran's Chocolates, and various breweries.

The modern exterior of the Bainbridge Island Museum of Art

6 Kubota Garden

Worth the detour to Renton, this beautiful Japanese garden *(see p45)* was founded by Japanese-born Fujitaro Kubota in 1927, and opened to the public in 1987. His work was interrupted by his internment during World War II; the grounds are still maintained by the Kubota family. This rarely crowded site is especially magical when the cherry blossoms are in flower in springtime.

7 Seattle Pinball Museum

MAP L6 ■ 508 Maynard Ave S ■ (206) 623-0759 ■ Adm ■ www.seattlepinballmuseum.com

Visitors cannot play the 1939 game on display in the window, but they are free to use almost everything else in the two-floor collection – and play is included with the price of admission. The atmosphere is lively and energetic owing to all the flashing lights, ringing bells, and rolling counters.

8 Mimosas Cabaret

MAP L3 ■ (206) 325-6492 ■ 1118 E Pike St ■ Open 1–4pm Sun ■ www.unicornseattle.com/mimosascabaret

Visit for the brunch buffet, drag queens, and accelerated versions of popular Broadway musicals. This Sunday afternoon extravaganza is for anyone who enjoys cabaret and stiff drinks. It is raunchy fun for the open minded (and those aged 21 and over). Be sure to bring some small change to tip the performers. Reservations are recommended.

9 Bainbridge Island Museum of Art

MAP N2 ■ 550 Winslow Way E ■ (206) 842-4451 ■ www.biartmuseum.org

Take the ferry downtown and get off at Bainbridge Island to visit this museum, which showcases the work of local Pacific Northwest artists. It's a very short walk from the museum to the quaint village of Winslow for some shopping and refreshments.

10 Lake View Cemetery

The final resting place of martial arts master, Bruce Lee, and his son, Brandon, this cemetery *(see p80)* is often thronged by fans looking to pay homage to their idol. The graves of many famous Seattleites, including founder Arthur A. Denny and department store magnate John W. Nordstrom, are also located here.

The Lees' grave, Lake View Cemetery

Children's Attractions

1 Seattle Children's Museum

MAP H2 ▪ 305 Harrison St ▪ (260) 441-1768 ▪ Open 10am–5pm Tue–Sun ▪ Adm ▪ www.thechildrens museum.org

In the heart of Seattle Center, this museum contains interesting galleries and hands-on studio spaces that stimulate children's imaginations. The Global Village reveals lifestyles of Japan, Ghana, and the Philippines, and the Bijou Theatre invites young performers to dress up and act.

2 Space Needle

A 41-second glass-elevator ride rockets you up to the observation deck for unforgettable views *(see p15)*. Visitors can also enjoy an exhilarating virtual reality bungee jump, snack on a range of delicious treats at the observation level café, or watch the rotating glass floor in The Loupe.

3 International Fountain

MAP H2 ▪ 305 Harrison St ▪ (206) 684-7200

During any festival and all through summer, the fountain draws scores of frolicking children. Weather permitting, kids play in the majestic arcs of water projecting out and up from the spherical base, all to music.

International Fountain on a sunny day

Children's Film Festival performers

4 Children's Film Festival Seattle

MAP M3 ▪ 1515 12th Ave ▪ (206) 329-2629 ▪ Adm ▪ www.childrens filmfestivalseattle.org

This two–week event allows young people and families to enjoy and even judge new feature films. It is held annually, January to February.

5 Seattle Pinball Museum

Kids can play as many games as they like for a single admission price at this fun-filled museum *(see p49)*. There are more than 50 games, some dating back to the 1960s.

6 Museum of Flight

Piquing scientific curiosity with fascinating exhibits, this museum *(see p41)* takes visitors on a journey from the earliest days of aviation to the Space Age. It also provides insightful outreach programs for children.

7 Toy Stores

Magic Mouse Toys: MAP K5; 603 1st Ave; (206) 682-8097 ■ **Snapdoodle Toys:** MAP P2; 120 N 85th St; (206) 782-0098

The city's much-loved local toy stores enjoy a loyal following due to their range of enticing products. Browse through the jam-packed aisles at Top Ten Toys and Magic Mouse Toys.

8 Artists at Play

MAP D4 ■ Seattle Center, 305 Harrison St

This playground, featuring a 30-ft (9-m) climbing tower, a labyrinth, and a human-powered accessible carousel, is great fun for children. There are also musical instruments, sound and listening stations, and play mounds.

Ride the Ducks amphibious vehicle

9 Ride the Ducks

MAP H2 ■ 516 Broad St ■ (206) 441-3825 ■ www.ridethe ducksofseattle.com

These amphibious vehicles from World War II offer an offbeat excursion around downtown, the Pike Place Market, Pioneer Square, Fremont, and Lake Union's houseboats.

10 Northwest Puppet Center

MAP P2 ■ 9123 15th Ave NE ■ (206) 523-2579 ■ www.nwpuppet.org

Established by the Carter Family Marionettes in 1986, this center has a museum and a library. It features more than 250 annual performances and troupe tours, and also sponsors educational outreach programs.

TOP 10 HOTELS WITH SWIMMING POOLS

The Fairmont Olympic Hotel

1 Fairmont Olympic Hotel
The indoor pool and spa are just two of many amenities here *(see p116)*.

2 Seattle Marriott Waterfront
This attractive waterfront hotel offers a heated indoor as well as outdoor pool, with views of Puget Sound *(see p117)*.

3 Hotel Ballard
MAP C2 ■ 5216 Ballard Ave NW ■ (206) 789-5012
Guests get full access to the Olympic Athletic Club next door and its two swimming pools.

4 Sheraton Seattle
MAP K4 ■ 1400 6th Ave ■ (206) 621-9000
Parents may prefer idle moments in the wine bar, but the hotel also has a heated indoor pool for all ages.

5 The Westin Seattle
The indoor pool here *(see p117)* is an all-weather plus, as is the fitness center.

6 University Inn
Families will appreciate the free breakfast buffet and outdoor pool *(see p117)*.

7 Travelodge Seattle Center
Amenities at this budget-friendly option *(see p119)* include an outdoor pool, hot tub, and complimentary breakfast.

8 Warwick Seattle Hotel
This family-friendly hotel *(see p119)* in Belltown has many 24-hour extras and an excellent pool.

9 The Maxwell Hotel Seattle
Well-located, dog-friendly hotel *(see p119)* with a pool and cycle hire.

10 Silver Cloud Inn
MAP M4 ■ 1100 Broadway ■ (206) 325-1400
Take advantage of this inn's pool and complimentary shuttles to downtown.

Performing Arts Venues

Glitzy foyer of the 20th-century Paramount Theatre

1 Paramount Theatre
MAP K3 ▪ 911 Pine St ▪ (206) 682-1414 ▪ www.stgpresents.org

One of the most treasured theaters in town, the restored Paramount dates from 1928 and exudes the charm of the popular Beaux Arts style of its period. Today, it presents Broadway shows, jazz and rock concerts, and dance performances.

2 Moore Theatre

Built in 1907, the grand lobby and halls of Seattle's oldest theater (see p74) is full of mosaics, stained glass, and woodcarvings. In 1974, it was placed on the National Register of Historic Places. It also serves as a base for new rock bands.

3 ACT Theatre/ Kreielsheimer Place
MAP K4 ▪ 700 Union St ▪ (206) 292-7676 ▪ www.acttheatre.org

Housed in the beautifully refurbished Kreielsheimer Place (formerly the Eagles Auditorium), the long-running A Contemporary Theatre (ACT) showcases modern playwrights. Inside, the cultural center contains four performance spaces, administrative offices, rehearsal spaces, and scene and costume shops.

4 Seattle Repertory Theatre

The Bagley Wright Hall at the Seattle Center belongs to the nonprofit Seattle Repertory Theatre (see p15). It is the flagship, and largest of the company's three performance venues. Over time, the Rep has received numerous accolades, confirming its reputation for producing classic and contemporary plays of high literary standards.

5 Washington Hall
MAP M5 ▪ 153 14th Ave ▪ www.washingtonhall.org

Built in 1907 in a Mission Revival style, Washington Hall has become one of Seattle's most loved venues, having hosted music legends such as Jimi Hendrix and Billie Holiday. Today, it continues to host concerts, theater, and events.

6 McCaw Hall

In 2003, Seattle's original opera house underwent a massive transformation to become McCaw Hall (see pp14–15). Built for no less than $127 million, this plush 2,900-seat auditorium, with state-of-the-art acoustics and amenities, is home to the Seattle Opera and Pacific Northwest Ballet.

An opera in session at McCaw Hall

7 5th Avenue Theatre
MAP K4 ■ 1308 5th Ave
■ (206) 625-1900 ■ www.5th
avenuetheatre.org

Established in 1926 as a vaudeville venue, 5th Avenue boasts an ornate imperial Chinese design inspired by Beijing's Forbidden City. It is Seattle's home for touring musical theater.

8 Broadway Performance Hall

Victor Steinbrueck, who helped preserve Pike Place Market (see pp12–13), was also instrumental in saving this auditorium (see p24) from demolition. Its repertoire includes film festivals, music and dance recitals, and off-the-wall theater.

Dance performance, Sky Church

9 Sky Church
MAP H2 ■ 325 5th Ave N
■ (206) 770-2700 ■ www.mopop.org

Located inside the Museum of Pop Culture (see pp14–15), this great performance venue has a 85-ft- (26-m-) high room with computer-controlled light systems, a huge video screen, and 48,000 watts of surround-sound.

10 Benaroya Hall
MAP K4 ■ 200 University St
■ (206) 215-4747 ■ www.seattle
symphony.org

This bastion of culture is the city's first venue designed exclusively for music performances. It is also home to the Seattle Symphony. The 2,500-seat Mark Taper auditorium is well known for its acoustics. A 540-seat hall is used for smaller concerts.

TOP 10 CINEMAS

Neptune theater hall

1 Neptune
MAP E2 ■ 1303 NE 45th St
■ (206) 682-1414
Built in 1921, this place has a nautical motif and movie-palace grandeur.

2 Central Cinema
MAP F4 ■ 1411 21st Ave
■ (206) 328-3230
A one-of-a-kind theatre with food and cocktail service available on site.

3 Northwest Film Forum
An independent cinema and studio that promotes new work (see p80).

4 Regal Meridian 16
MAP K4 ■ 1501 7th Ave ■ (844) 462-7342
Watch Hollywood's latest releases here.

5 Seattle Outdoor Cinema
MAP J2 ■ 101 Westlake Ave N
■ www.seattleoutdoormovies.com
Pack a picnic in the summers to take to this walk-in, outdoor theater.

6 Majestic Bay
MAP B1 ■ 2044 NW Market St
■ (206) 781-2229
A vintage theater with modern luxuries.

7 Rendezvous/Jewel Box
This Belltown bar (see p74) seats only a few die-hard fans of independent film.

8 Grand Illusion
MAP E2 ■ 1403 NE 50th St
■ (206) 523-3935
Shows the best of avant-garde cinema.

9 SIFF Cinema Egyptian
MAP L3 ■ 805 E Pine St
■ (206) 324-9996
A classic single-screen cinema (see p25) with a focus on indie films.

10 Varsity
MAP E2 ■ 4329 University Way NE
■ (206) 632-7218
The Varsity has thrived since 1940.

Nightlife

① Dimitriou's Jazz Alley
MAP J3 ▪ 2033 6th Ave
▪ **(206) 441-9729**

A solid anchor in the Seattle music scene, Dimitriou's Jazz Alley has been bringing the best jazz, swing, and blues musicians to the Pacific Northwest since 1979. Big acts that have performed here include Taj Mahal, Eartha Kitt, The Count Basie Orchestra, and Dr. John. There are dinner shows and music-only shows.

Performance at Dimitriou's Jazz Alley

② El Corazón
MAP L3 ▪ 109 Eastlake Ave E
▪ **(206) 262-0482**

Formerly known as Graceland, El Corazón proudly flaunts its roots as a crusty, smoky rock club. It is a mecca for many of the area's rock bands.

③ The Triple Door
MAP J4 ▪ 216 Union St
▪ **(206) 838-4333**

In the space of a former 1920s-era vaudeville theater, upscale audiences soak up the best of live jazz, rock, blues, and cabaret while enjoying Pan-Asian drinks and cuisine.

④ The Showbox
MAP J4 ▪ 1426 1st Ave
▪ **(206) 628-0221**

An elegant Art Deco room founded in the 1900s, The Showbox has state-of-the-art audio and lighting, and has been used as a concert hall and comedy club. Artists as dissimilar as the Mills Brothers, the Ramones, and Al Jolson have performed here. Now, the 1,000-seat venue hosts rock and hip-hop acts.

⑤ Nectar Lounge
MAP D2 ▪ 412 N 36th St
▪ **(206) 632-2020**

A happening Fremont club, Nectar features live music seven nights a week, ranging from indie to hip-hop, reggae to dance, folk, funk, punk, and more. It is host to a good range of national and local acts. There are three bars and an attractive outdoor patio with a fireplace, making this a favorite spot for younger Seattleites. Bar food and a great selection of pizzas are also available.

⑥ Chop Suey
This club *(see p84)* dominates the smoke-filled, hard rock scene on Capitol Hill, but does so with style and flair. Glowing red lights and lanterns shed a little light, while Bruce Lee imagery adds to the kitschy theme. Most of the acts are local or regional rock outfits, although hip-hop rules on Sunday nights.

Kitsch interior at Chop Suey

Revelers partying at Neumos

7 Neumos
MAP M3 ▪ 925 E Pike St
▪ (206) 709-9467

Previously known as Moe's, this is Capitol Hill's trendiest music venue. The club offers indie and classic rock, plus DJ dance nights.

8 Tractor Tavern
MAP B2 ▪ 5213 Ballard Ave NW
▪ (206) 789-3599

A bastion of great music, this place thrives as an alternative to clubs elsewhere in Seattle that are known for hard rock acts. Conversely, the Tractor primarily books bands with repertoire in the vein of country and western, rockabilly, bluegrass, or musicians who seamlessly fuse all those styles into something original.

9 Gallery 1412
MAP E5 ▪ 1412 18th Ave
▪ (206) 324-6822

Gallery 1412 is a collectively owned musical arts venue with an imposing artistic vision. The award-winning curators book acts dedicated to experimental music in a no-frills setting. Patrons listen and learn about contemporary composition, electro-acoustic and electronic music, improvization, and jazz.

10 Sunset Tavern
MAP B1 ▪ 5433 Ballard Ave NW
▪ (206) 784-4880

This tavern is primarily an outlet for start-up bands of the ear-shattering punk rock persuasion. The room's red decor and lighting seems to take inspiration from a Victorian bordello.

TOP 10 LOCAL MICROBREWERIES

1 Redhook Brewery
MAP E4 ▪ 714 E Pike St
▪ (206) 823-3026
One of the top breweries since 1981.

2 Hale's Ales Brewery
Savor the brews and grub here (see p95).

3 Maritime Pacific Brewing Company
MAP C2 ▪ 1111 NW Ballard Way
▪ (206) 782-6181
Order a pint of Nightwatch here.

4 Elliott Bay Brewing Company
MAP A6 ▪ 4720 California Ave SW
▪ (206) 932-8695
This is West Seattle's bastion of microbrews and pub fare.

5 McMenamins Six Arms
MAP E4 ▪ 300 E Pike St ▪ (206) 223-1698
Six Arms is a popular branch of the McMenamins microbrew chain.

6 Elysian Brewing Company
The Hill's best pub (see p84) makes its own legendary brews.

7 Old Stove Brewing
MAP J4 ▪ 1901 Western Ave ▪ (206) 602-6120
Enjoy views of the bay while sipping on craft beers and snacking on oysters.

8 Big Time Brewery & Alehouse
MAP E2 ▪ 4133 University Way NE
▪ (206) 545-4509
Sample handcrafted ales here.

9 Mac & Jack's
MAP P2 ▪ 17825 NE 65th St, Redmond ▪ (425) 558-9697
Try their great African Amber.

10 Pike Brewing Company
MAP J4 ▪ 1415 1st Ave ▪ (206) 622-6044
Best for microbrews, pub food, or for purchasing brewing supplies.

Exterior of Pike Brewing Company

🔟 Restaurants

Tasteful decor and plush furnishings at Lark

1 Lark
Located in a converted 1917 warehouse with high ceilings, chef John Sundstrom's Lark (see p85) is one of the Pacific Northwest's most lauded restaurants, known for working with local farmers to provide seasonal dishes. The menu features delicious and fresh small plates of locally produced cheese, vegetables, charcuterie, and fish.

2 Metropolitan Grill
One of Seattle's most loved and traditional steakhouses (see p77) draws in a faithful group of politicians and corporate attorneys every day. Portions are typically huge, especially for salads, appetizers, and baked potatoes, so bring lots of friends for sharing. The award-winning wine list is worth a perusal, and there are experienced sommeliers for help.

Wagyu beef dish, Metropolitan Grill

3 Ray's Boathouse & Café
This Ballard waterfront restaurant (see p101) has two dining rooms. The café caters to happy-hour revelers, families, and casual diners, while the boathouse has reservation-only seating. Both menus include the freshest Dungeness crab, oysters, and wild Alaskan salmon.

4 Café Juanita
MAP P2
■ 9702 NE 120th Place, Kirkland ■ (425) 823-1505 ■ Closed L, Sun & Mon ■ $$$
This award-winning restaurant in Kirkland is renowned for its passion for Northern Italian food and wine. The lengthy menu reflects the kitchen's commitment toward organic, sustainable ingredients. Exceptional service and a calm, classy dining room complete the experience.

5 Canlis
Treat your eyes and palate to a special dinner at Canlis (see p95). Specialties include Alaska halibut, Wagyu-style tenderloin, Dungeness crab, and a comprehensive and well-curated wine selection. For an even more memorable occasion, consider booking the private cache room for two, and order in advance to ensure a serving of the luscious chocolate lava cake. Reserve ahead.

6 Lecosho
MAP J5 ■ 89 University St ■ (206) 623-2101 ■ $$$
Set on the Harbor Steps, this spot is a long-time favorite. It has a simple and elegant menu that offers local meats and produce. The outdoor heated patio is a fun spot to relax after a long day.

7 The Herbfarm
MAP P2 ■ 14590 NE 145th St, Woodinville ■ (425) 485-5300 ■ Closed D Sun–Wed ■ $$$
Dining at this Eastside restaurant requires time, money, as well as an appreciation of the culinary arts.

For a key to restaurant price ranges see p77

Acclaimed chef Chris Weber's kitchen often uses ingredients from the restaurant's gardens and farm. Creative menus include a nine-course dinner of Northwest foods, served with five or six matched wines (non-alcoholic options are also available). Be sure to reserve well in advance.

8 Matt's in the Market
MAP J4 ▪ 94 Pike St, Suite 32 ▪ (206) 467-7909 ▪ Closed Mon, Tue & Sun D ▪ $$$

A Pike Place institution for fresh seafood and upscale American cuisine, this bustling restaurant on the second floor has huge windows that provide views of the entire market. The lunch menu is the main draw here, which features its popular fried catfish sandwich.

9 Ben Paris
MAP J4 ▪ 130 Pike St ▪ (206) 513-7303 ▪ $$$

Housed in the State Hotel, this casual, bustling place in the heart of downtown is known for its creative cocktail menu, fresh Pacific Northwest cuisine, and fast, friendly service. Try the fried chicken sandwich and Wagyu burgers for lunch.

10 The Walrus and the Carpenter

Try the steak tartare and the freshly caught oysters, washed down with great cocktails at this buzzing, trendy seafood restaurant (see p101). Expect to have to line up on weekends; there are no reservations.

The Walrus and the Carpenter

TOP 10 CAFÉS

Interior of Fremont Coffee Company

1 Fremont Coffee Company
MAP D2 ▪ 459 N 36th ▪ (206) 632-3633
Superb coffee and tasty wraps.

2 Bauhaus Strong Coffee
MAP B1 ▪ 2001 NW Market St ▪ (206) 453-3068
Home-roasted coffee and pastries.

3 Caffé Ladro
MAP E4 ▪ 435 15th Ave E ▪ (206) 267-0551
A local chain with excellent espressos.

4 Zeitgeist
MAP K6 ▪ 171 S Jackson ▪ (206) 583-0497
This place makes exceptional espresso and also sponsors art shows.

5 Little Oddfellows
Café in the Elliott Bay Book Co. (see p83).

6 Herkimer Coffee
MAP P2 ▪ 7320 Greenwood N ▪ (206) 784-0202
A tastefully designed coffee shop.

7 Lighthouse Roasters
MAP D2 ▪ 400 N 43rd ▪ (206) 634-3140
Rich drinks are made from freshly roasted coffee beans.

8 Café Allegro
MAP E2 ▪ 4214 University Way NE ▪ (206) 633-3030
Keeps students, professors, and locals stoked on perfectly brewed coffee.

9 Café Besalu
MAP B1 ▪ 5909 24th Ave NW ▪ (206) 789-1463
This European-style café lures foodies with its gourmet pastries.

10 Espresso Vivace
A Northern Italian-style cozy café (see p84) serving aromatic blends.

🔟 Stores and Shopping Centers

1 5th Avenue Boutiques

MAP K4

A collection of boutiques between Union and Spring Streets caters to customers for whom price is no object. Louis Vuitton, Michael Kors, and Fox's Seattle, are among the best stops for fine gems, jewelry, and high fashion galore.

The Apple Store at University Village

2 Filson

MAP D6 ▪ 1741 1st Ave S ▪ (206) 622-3147

Ever since the advent of the Gold Rush, this Seattle-based outfitter, established in 1897, has been a popular choice for high-quality outdoor gear and clothing. Much of its merchandise is still crafted in this store, Filson's original outlet in Seattle. Factory tours are available free of cost, but require advance booking.

3 Nordstrom

John W. Nordstrom's (see p37) shoe store, opened with his Alaskan gold rush earnings in 1901, is now synonymous with impeccable service and quality merchandise. Hunting for fine apparel, exquisite handbags, elegant shoes, or other accessories can be exhausting, so step into the fancy in-store spa and salon to relax. Afterwards, grab a bite at one of its many cafés and restaurants (see p76).

Dresses at a bridal shop in Nordstrom

4 University Village

MAP F2 ▪ 2623 NE University Village St ▪ (206) 523-0622

Situated just east of the University of Washington, this urban shopping center has lovely landscaped walkways, fountains, restaurants, and stores that no longer attract just the resident graduate student population. Shops include an Apple Store, Nike Running, Warby Parker, RH Gallery, Madewell, and Din Tai Fung.

5 Westlake Center

This shopping mall (see p76) has a four-tiered glass-enclosed atrium stacked with small locally-based shops, chain stores, and a food court. Made in Washington, Fireworks, Zara, Nordstrom Rack, Lush, and Saks 5th Avenue Outlet are well worth a visit. Outside, the center attracts workers on break, and also serves as a venue for seasonal concerts and events.

6 North of the Market to Belltown

MAP J4

A stroll along First and Second avenues in the Belltown area leads to this ultrahip shopping destination. There are boutique shoe stores, upscale bathroom fixtures and furnishing stores, art galleries, and many other intriguing stores for curious shoppers. And, when a rest is needed, there is no shortage of restaurants, coffee shops, or bars.

(7) Wallingford Center
MAP D2 ■ 1815 N 45th St
■ (206) 517-7773

For a real taste of the charming Wallingford neighborhood, explore the variety of local commerce along 45th Street, such as restaurants and shops, plus the Wallingford Center, an early-19th-century elementary school. To catch a quick break in between shopping, stop at Trophy Cupcakes and indulge in a freshly baked cupcake or two.

(8) Melrose Market
Housed in a series of former automotive repair buildings, this chic upscale indoor-outdoor market (see p83) includes several trendy restaurants, a meat market, home decor and gift shops, as well as a clothing boutique and spirits shop. Post shopping, tuck into some freshly shucked oysters along with a refreshing drink at Taylor Shellfish (1521 Melrose Ave).

(9) Pacific Place
The huge, multi-level Pacific Place (see p76) is the crown jewel of Seattle's retail shopping centers. Stores include Tiffany & Co., Coach, Kate Spade, Aveda, Lululemon, L'Occitane, and J. Crew. The top level has an 11-screen AMC Theatre complex and several fine gourmet restaurants. To top it off, there is also a skybridge connection to the Nordstrom flagship store. During

the month of December, the festive "snow fall" inside the Atrium is a prime attraction and attracts large numbers of visitors.

(10) Westfield Southcenter
MAP P3 ■ 2800 Southcenter Mall ■ (206) 246-0423

With more than 200 shops and services, this is the largest shopping center in the Pacific Northwest. Key stores include JCPenney, Nordstrom, Sears, J.Crew, Abercrombie & Fitch, Pandora, Bebe, Macy's, and Sephora. There are also plenty of restaurants, a food court facing Mount Rainier, a rainforest-themed play area for kids, and a 16-screen AMC movie theater. The mall is located in the suburban city of Tukwila, close to the airport.

Interior of the large Pacific Place, one of Seattle's top malls

🔟 Seattle for Free

Washington Park Arboretum

1 Washington Park Arboretum and Japanese Garden

The plants here range from sprawling big leaf maples to the water lilies in Duck Bay, which is also a good place for turtle spotting. There is an entry fee for the Japanese Garden *(see p45)* but the rest of the grounds are free to explore. It is especially nice in fall when the leaves change.

2 Center for Wooden Boats Sunday Public Sailing

Sprit boats, steamboats, electric boats, schooners, ketches, yawls, and yachts: the fleet varies, but they sail every Sunday. It is first come first served, so show up early *(see p40)*.

3 Discovery Park

Trails zigzag across the bluffs of the park and down to the rocky beach on Puget Sound *(see pp32–3)*, offering gorgeous views across the water to the Olympic Mountains.

4 Northwest Folklife Festival

Enjoy three days of international food, music, storytelling, and theater at this free festival *(see p42)*. The aim is to celebrate the communities that make up the Pacific Northwest and the arts they create. It can get busy, but it is always fun.

5 Ballard Fish Ladder
MAP C2 ■ 3015 NW 54th St ■ (206) 783-7059

Forward thinking conservationist Hiram M. Chittenden understood that the building of a passageway to help ships reach the inland shipyards would disrupt the salmon migration, so he built this underwater staircase to help them. The peak season for salmon viewing in the underwater gallery is June to September.

6 First Thursday Art Walk
MAP K5 ■ Pioneer Square ■ www.pioneersquare.org/ experiences/first-thursday-art-walk

Explore Seattle's great contemporary art scene on the first Thursday of every month, when all the Pioneer Square galleries open their doors to introduce new exhibitions and artists. Pick up a gallery guide at any of the Pioneer Square galleries and enjoy the people-watching.

7 Frye Art Museum

This small, privately funded museum *(see p40)* is situated on First Hill. It has frequently changing displays of contemporary art, and a salon-style permanent collection. Contrary to the traditional nature of the permanent collection, the temporary exhibits are often bold and avant-garde. There is also a good café on site for refreshments.

Frye Art Museum collection

⑧ Gates Foundation Discovery Center

MAP H2 ■ 440 5th Avenue N
■ (206) 709-3100 ■ www.
discovergates.org

This center is dedicated to exploring the philanthropic endeavors of Bill and Melinda Gates. The hands-on exhibits here invite visitors to think of dynamic solutions to real-world problems concerning poverty, education, and health.

⑨ Central Library

Architect Rem Koolhaas designed the angular, glass-and-steel central library *(see p72)*, which is home to site-specific public art, including an acid-green wall backed with video displays, and a letter-press-inspired floor. No library card is required, and there are lots of free events, too.

Modern design of the Central Library

⑩ Olympic Sculpture Park

This open-air sculpture garden has monumental works of art *(see p17)*, including an enormous Richard Serra installation that kids seem to love, and a whimsical type-writer eraser by Claes Oldenburg. It is a diverting outdoor space, especially on summer evenings.

TOP 10 BUDGET TIPS

Seattle's light rail

1 Skip the Car
Get an ORCA card and use public transit. Light rail runs from the airport, through downtown Seattle, and to the University of Washington.

2 Check Out a Food Court
Crossroads Mall, Uwajimaya Market, and Seattle Center offer good food that costs less than it does in a formal restaurant.

3 Go on Thursday
Many of Seattle's museums are free (excluding special exhibitions) on the first Thursday of every month.

4 Get a CityPASS
This pass allows entry to Seattle's most popular attractions, saving money.

5 Find a Happy Hour
On weekdays, bars and restaurants have discounted menus between 4pm and 6pm.

6 Picnic
Check out Pike Place and farmers' markets across the city, then stock up on local goodies and head for a park.

7 Stay in a Neighborhood
Centrally located hotels are more convenient, but money can be saved by choosing a place farther out.

8 Check *The Stranger*
Seattle's weekly independent arts and culture newspaper lists the low- and no-cover bars, plus great free events.

9 Head for a Food Truck
Enjoy a quick bite at one of the many food trucks offering local delicacies, which are value for money and delightful lunch options.

10 Be a Bookworm
World-class writers read and tell stories in Seattle bookstores for free. Often there is a top notch café on site.

Festivals and Parades

① Seattle Improvised Music Festival (SIMF)

Feb ■ www.waywardmusic.org

The largest and longest-running music festival of its kind anywhere, SIMF is dedicated to improvised music performances. Local performers join eclectic international musicians to improvise sets that defy categorization, but always impress.

The stage at Bumbershoot

② Bumbershoot

Labor Day weekend ■ www. bumbershoot.com

Performers from all over the world converge for this festival (see p14) for three days packed with concerts, theater productions, independent film screenings, and literary events.

③ Seattle Maritime Festival

May ■ www.seattlemaritime101.com

Enthusiasts of tugboats and ships flock to this festival. It makes for a free, fun, and family-friendly way to learn how the working waterfront has become a major factor in the city's economy and culture. The fair centers around the Bell Street Pier, which is a short walk north from the Seattle Aquarium (see p16) on Pier 59. An exciting and fun highlight is the tugboat race on Elliott Bay.

④ University District Street Fair

May ■ www.udistrictstreetfair.org

Dating from 1970, Seattle's first street fair stretches over ten blocks of "The Ave" and its sidestreets.

Crafts booths, food vendors, and local rock music performances attract families from all over town and beyond.

⑤ Northwest Folklife Festival

Memorial Day weekend ■ www. nwfolklife.org

A free and fun-filled celebration (see p60) of the Pacific Northwest's multi-cultural music, dance, and arts and crafts, Folklife is a magnet for old (as well as new) hippies in the region.

⑥ Seattle International Film Festival (SIFF)

May–Jun ■ www.siff.net

One of the most respected film festivals in the US, SIFF screens more than 400 new works from at least 60 countries. Even midnight showings of cult films sell out, and notable directors attend screenings.

⑦ Fremont Fair Solstice Parade

Late Jun ■ www.fremontfair.com

All floats at this parade must be entirely human-powered, thereby encouraging Fremont's arts community to innovate. Crews propel samba bands, dancers, and rock quartets using battery-operated amplifiers.

The Fremont Fair Solstice parade

Seattle Pride March performer

8 Seattle Pride March
Late Jun ▪ www.seattle pride.org

Sponsored by the non-profit Seattle Out & Proud, the lively Seattle Pride March runs from Westlake Park to Seattle Center and attracts huge crowds. Expect colorful floats, dancing, and the very popular "Dykes That Ride", a motorcycle outfit whose members come together to challenge cultural stereotypes and expectations.

9 Seafair Weekend Festival
Early Aug ▪ www.seafair.com

A parade along 4th Avenue is a highlight of Seafair, a celebration of maritime and aviation history. Events include displays from Navy's Blue Angels F/A-18 fighter pilots, BMX bike stunts, hydroplane racing, wakeboarding competitions, and a classic car show.

10 Earshot Jazz Festival
Oct–Nov ▪ www.earshot.org

The shoestring staff at the nonprofit Earshot Jazz Festival present a well-respected event. The festivals have consistently showcased successful and emerging jazz artists, enriching the Seattle community at large.

TOP 10 TRADITIONAL FIESTAS

1 Têt Festival
A colorful beginning in late January marks the Vietnamese Lunar New Year.

2 Irish Week Festival
Two days of Irish culture around St. Patrick's Day in mid-March.

3 Seattle Cherry Blossom and Japanese Cultural Festival
Dance, music, martial arts, and tea ceremonies are the highlights of this mid-April fair.

4 Festival Sundiata
The longest-running African American festival in the Pacific Northwest features local entertainment, art, food, and music.

5 Pagdiriwang Philippine Festival
Philippine independence is marked in early June with a festival of dance, film, drama, and culinary arts.

6 BrasilFest
Expect infectious rhythms, dance, and spicy flavors when celebrating this Brazilian Folklore Day in late August.

7 Festa Italiana
This late September festival is all about Italian-style fun and food.

8 Indigenous People Festival
Usually taking place in mid-October, this festival celebrates American Indian and Alaska Native cultures with dance, music, art, and food.

9 Día de los Muertos
Mexicans honor the loved ones that they have lost with altars, artwork, food, and music in early November.

10 Hmong New Year
November marks the end of harvest, a time for relaxing and preparing special foods for the Hmong community.

Dragon costume at Têt Festival

Day Trips: Islands and Historic Towns

1 Vashon Island
MAP N3

This island's gentle, two-lane roads make it a favorite for both cyclists and motorcyclists looking for a countryside getaway. Board the Fauntleroy Ferry *(see p104)* to visit the island's estates, art galleries, berry and llama farms, and to experience the ambiance of a small country town.

Point Robinson Light, Vashon Island

2 Victoria, BC
MAP N4

Catch a ferry or seaplane to British Columbia's capital, Victoria. Founded as a fur-trading post of the Hudson's Bay Company in 1843, it has become a favorite destination for Anglophiles who line up at the grand Fairmont Empress Hotel for traditional tea and cakes. Other attractions here include the Inner Harbor, the Royal British Columbia Museum, and Butchart Gardens – an amazing collection of flora planted in a sprawling former quarry.

3 Whidbey Island
MAP P1

The longest island in the western United States, Whidbey Island offers ample waterfront real estate, making it vacation-home central. The island's six state parks, seaside villages, and historic forts attract weekend crowds. It also serves as the perfect location for the largest US Navy air base in the area. The sign here reads, "Pardon our noise, it's the sound of freedom".

4 Port Townsend
MAP N1

On the northeast tip of the Olympic Peninsula, this idyllic seaport attracts artists and musicians. Known for its Victorian architecture, the town features Jefferson County Historical Society, Ann Starrett Mansion, Fort Worden Historical State Park, and Fire Bell Tower among its key sights. There is a bustling waterfront with stores, eateries, and a ferry terminal.

5 Olympia
MAP P6

Washington's state capital has a rich past, historic buildings, and a thriving youth culture. Highlights include the State Capitol Campus, with grounds designed by the Olmsted Brothers in 1928; the Evergreen State College; a farmers' market; the surrounding, mostly rural, Thurston County; and a number of art venues and theaters.

Washington State Capitol, Olympia

Tulip field in the Skagit Valley

6 La Conner and the Skagit Valley

MAP P4 ▪ (360) 466-4778 ▪ www.lovelaconner.com

Located around 70 miles (110 km) north of Seattle, Skagit Valley is the second-largest tulip-producing region in the world after the Netherlands. La Conner, a small community surrounded by flower fields is located some 20 miles (30 km) west of the Skagit Valley, and boasts several art galleries and cafés with lovely water views. One of the best ways to enjoy this corner of Washington is to rent a bicycle and pedal the area during peak flower season, typically in April. An annual tulip festival celebrates the blooms throughout the month.

7 Tacoma

MAP P3

Founded as a sawmill town in 1852, Tacoma is renowned for its historic buildings, which include the 1893 Italianate tower of Old City Hall. The magnificent, colorful Chihuly Bridge of Glass connects the Museum of Glass to downtown Tacoma and the imaginatively curated Washington State History Museum. Equally worth exploring are the impressive Tacoma Art Museum, and the Point Defiance Zoo and Aquarium, which has a Pacific Rim theme.

8 Bainbridge Island

MAP N2

The scenic ferry ride to Winslow on Bainbridge Island (from downtown Seattle's Pier 52) should be mandatory for tourists seeking an inspiring view of the Seattle skyline. The short stroll from the terminal to Winslow's charming waterfront stores and cafés has its own rewards.

9 Roslyn

MAP Q6

The model for Cicely, Alaska, in the Emmy-award-winning 1990s television show *Northern Exposure*, Roslyn has its own history unrelated to the quirky profiles offered in Hollywood's depiction. A 19th-century coal mining boom attracted immigrant workers from across Europe to the town. They set up distinct neighborhoods and kept the traditions of their home countries alive. Today, Roslyn is on the National Register of Historic Places.

10 Leavenworth

MAP Q5

In an effort to revive the struggling logging town, civic leaders remodeled buildings in 1960s Bavarian-style, turning it into a top tourist attraction. Today, the town bustles with festivals, art shows, and summer theater productions. Another attraction is the popular Leavenworth Nutcracker Museum and its 7,000 nutcrackers.

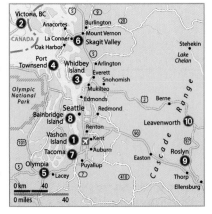

🔟 Day Trips: Mountain Getaways

Snoqualmie Falls' spectacular scenery

1 Snoqualmie Falls
MAP Q2

Indigenous tribes regard the dazzling Snoqualmie Falls as a sacred place. The 268-ft- (82-m-) high waterfall is beautifully divided by a convenient rock outcropping, and marks the end of the vast Cascade Plateau, where the Snoqualmie River begins its final descent to the sea, 40 miles (65 km) north at Everett. An observation deck and a steep path to the river allow for close-up breathtaking views.

2 Mount Rainier
MAP P6

This silent, snowcapped sentinel, the centerpiece of Mount Rainier National Park, is an awe-inspiring active volcano rising 14,410 ft (4,392 m) above sea level. The mountain is the most glaciated peak in the US. Its lower slopes are blanketed by forest, while higher up lie subalpine meadows.

3 Denny Creek
MAP Q5

Hiking near Snoqualmie Pass along I-90 is a popular spot for families with kids. The creek pours over a series of rocks and creates swimming pools.

4 Twin Falls
MAP Q5

Hikers in search of deep woods head to Olallie State Park, where a 3-mile (5-km) trail to Twin Falls awaits. The park features giant ferns and salmonberry, and some of the Cascades' few old-growth trees: one Douglas fir has a circumference of 14 ft (4 m).

5 Issaquah Alps
MAP Q3

These foothills west of the Cascades are remnants of mountains that predate the more-visited peaks to the east. Rattlesnake, Cougar, Tiger, and Squak mountains are the four main park areas that attract those seeking woodland walks without the altitude.

6 Mount Si
MAP Q3

Seattle's closest Cascade Mountain, Mount Si sits just past Issaquah. The hike is steep but not too difficult, and the views of the Snoqualmie Valley watershed and I-90 are rewarding.

7 Hurricane Ridge
MAP N5

Drive to this 5,242-ft (1,598-m) mountaintop at one of Olympic

The majestic Mount Rainier

National Park's most-visited sites. The paved routes bring visitors to one of the best 360-degree Alpine overlooks. During winter, when the snowpack is deep, the roads remain open for skiers and snowshoers.

8 Staircase Rapids
MAP N5

The ferry crossing and subsequent scenic drive along the Hood Canal enhance the journey to these rapids. The popular route inches close to the fast-flowing Skokomish River as it pours down the eastern slopes of the Olympic Range en route to Lake Cushman. Kingfishers and harlequin ducks, and giant salamanders can be sighted along the 2-mile (3-km) loop.

Kingfisher, Staircase Rapids

9 Tonga Ridge
MAP Q5

The 6-mile (10-km) trail in the Alpine Lakes Wilderness offers a pleasant walk through forests where visitors can go wild-berry picking (when in season). Meadows bloom in late spring, and mountain scenery abounds.

10 Big Four Ice Caves
MAP P5

Global warming has taken a toll on ice caves, but the attraction at the base of 6,180-ft (1,880-m) Big Four Mountain in the North Cascades is still vital. Hike the 1-mile (1.6-km) trail off the Mountain Loop Highway to the Ice Caves, the unusual result of Alpine avalanches and climate conditions impacting the ice field.

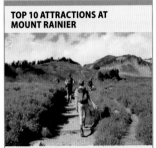

TOP 10 ATTRACTIONS AT MOUNT RAINIER

Hikers walking through Paradise

1 Paradise
This area leads to wildflower-filled meadows, and trails starting at 5,400-ft (1,646-m) to moraines and majestic views of the Nisqually Glacier.

2 Sunrise
Solo hikers will have lots of company on this busy trail, reachable by car.

3 Summit Climb
A round trip to the crater and back requires training, professional gear, and takes a few days. Those who are not seasoned climbers should rent a guide or go with a group.

4 Family Day Hikes
Dozens of trails for family day trips and picnics are available; try one out near the Carbon River entrance.

5 Wonderland Trail
This 93-mile (149-km) trail through several mini-ecosystems around the mountain is ideal for serious backpackers with weeks to spare.

6 Cloud Lid
Rainier's cloud cover often resembles a flying saucer hovering above the peak.

7 Glacial Melting
Climate changes have decreased the area of Rainier's permanent snowcap and has facilitated glacial retreats.

8 Jökulhlaups and Lahars
These glacial floods and debris flows, typical of Rainier, can move at speeds of up to 60 mph (96 kmph).

9 Sleeping Giant
Experts agree that it is a question of when, and not if, Mount Rainier's active volcano will blow again.

10 Trail of the Shadows
A refreshing nature trail that snakes through a setting of alder and cedar trees and vibrant mineral springs.

Seattle
Area by Area

Tlingit totem pole in
Pioneer Square Park

🔟 Downtown

What strikes many visitors to downtown Seattle is how easy it is to see the sights, since many of the key attractions lie within easy walking distance of one another. Bookended by Belltown to the north and Pioneer Square to the south, the sights in downtown can be explored on foot or using the city's excellent bus network. The waterfront boasts many attractions and seafood restaurants on its piers, as well as superb views. Although it is primarily a business district full of skyscrapers, downtown offers a wide range of entertainment options for visitors, such as gourmet restaurants, attractive shopping centers, upscale boutiques, and world-class galleries and art museums. Downtown is the perfect base from which to explore the city.

Seattle's Central Library

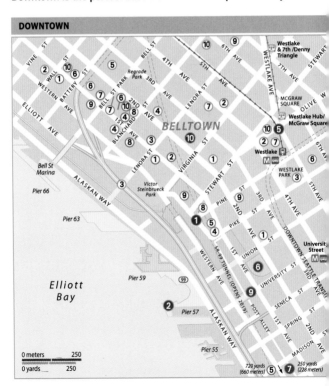

DOWNTOWN

1 Pike Place Market

Anyone descending on Pike Place Market *(see pp12–13)* can feel the rapid pulse of a scene that is all about the hustle. The lively market is famous for its salmon-throwing fish-mongers and street musicians who entertain market goers daily. Visitors typically come here to stroll by the innumerable stalls of seafood, fresh produce, crafts, and flower bouquets.

2 Seattle Great Wheel

At the end of Pier 57, on the Seattle waterfront, the Ferris wheel *(see p17)* sits 175 ft (53 m) above the pier and extends nearly 40 ft (12 m) over Elliott Bay. The 360-degree views from all of the 42 climate-controlled, fully enclosed gondolas are specta-cular. Each gondola accommodates eight people, and a ride on the wheel includes three rotations, each lasting

Seattle Great Wheel on Pier 57

between 12–20 minutes. For an extra cost, a VIP gondola is available, with leather seating and a glass bottom. Night rides are especially notable for the view of Seattle's lights.

3 Washington State Convention Center/ Freeway Park

MAP K4 ■ 705 Pike Street ■ (206) 694-5000 ■ www.wscc.com

Straddling the 10-lane Interstate 5 in a miraculous feat of engineering, the Washington State Convention Center is located within easy walking distance of the best stores, hotels, as well as restaurants in Seattle. Admire the 90-ft- (27-m-) wide glass canopy bridge that frames picturesque views to Elliott Bay and to the historic Pike-Pine neighborhood. Adjoining is the Freeway Park, where pretty blossoms delight visitors in spring, and soothing waterfalls mask the sounds of traffic flowing on all sides.

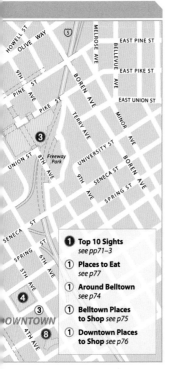

Washington State Convention Center

DENNY HILL REGRADE

Named after Arthur A. Denny, one of the city's founders, Denny Hill would have certainly become one of Seattle's most upscale neighborhoods, with magnificent views of the city, surrounding mountains, and water. However, in 1905, the city began removing and regrading the land to allow access to the rest of the city's neighborhoods. Today, this area spanning 50 square blocks, includes most of what is now called Belltown, and is occupied largely by sleek condos, trendy restaurants, as well as a number of social agencies.

④ Central Library

MAP K5 ▪ 1000 4th Ave ▪ Open 10am–8pm Mon–Sat (to 6pm Sat), noon–6pm Sun ▪ www.spl.org

Nearly 8,000 patrons per day benefit from more than 1.45 million books and reference materials, and more than 400 public computers at Seattle's main library (see p38). The art collection alone is valued at $1 million.

⑤ Seattle Center Monorail

For an adventurous and fun way to travel the 1 mile (1.6 km) between downtown's Westlake Center and the Seattle Center, hop aboard what engineers perceived as the future of mass transit (see p39). The first commercial monorail in the US was built as an attraction for the 1962 World's Fair, it still uses the original cars, and makes the short journey every ten minutes.

⑥ Seattle Art Museum

This museum (see pp30–31) houses major touring exhibitions, plus a stunning permanent collection of more than 25,000 works of ancient to modern art. In 2007, a light-filled addition to the sandstone-and-limestone edifice that houses the museum expanded the exhibition space. The SAM Shop sells unusual toys, jewelry, design books, and original artworks. The museum has two more branches: the Seattle Asian Art Museum (see p40), located in Volunteer Park, is home to a wide variety of Asian Art, while the Olympic Sculpture Park (see p17), at the north end of downtown, showcases unique sculptures in a stunning waterfront setting.

⑦ Pioneer Square

Find art galleries, intricate Victorian architecture, bookstores, and cafés in a constantly changing National Historic District (see pp18–19). Pioneer Square's small 20-block neighborhood ended up as Seattle's commercial center during the boom years of logging, fishing, railroads, and Klondike Gold Rush economies. A 75-minute underground tour offers a lively look at the 19th-century storefronts. A key sight here is the Smith Tower, and art lovers will enjoy an art walk that takes place on the first Thursday of each month (see p60).

Seattle Center Monorail train

8 Columbia Center
MAP K5 ■ 700 4th Ave
■ Observation deck: (206) 386-5564;
open May–Sep: 10am–10pm daily,
Oct–Apr: 10am–8pm daily; adm

The sleek, three-tiered skyscraper
(see p38) that dominates Seattle's
skyline might have been
even taller, but for an
order from the Federal
Aviation Administration
to reduce the final height.

Columbia Center tower

9 Harbor Steps
MAP J5

If you happen to be near the Seattle
Art Museum on 1st Avenue and need
to get down to the waterfront, try the
Harbor Steps. A street's abrupt end
has been turned into a wide-open
stairway, landscaped with planters
and water sculpture. The steps are
an ideal urban meeting spot, located
below a luxury apartment complex.
Countless restaurant and nightlife
options abound nearby.

10 Belltown
MAP J4

Pedestrians are welcomed here
with an explosion of stores, clubs,
cafés, luxury condos, and fine restaurants. This upscale neighborhood
was named after pioneer William N.
Bell. In those days, the area attracted
sailors on shore leave, artists seeking
inexpensive loft spaces, and ragtag
urban dwellers. However it was the
dot-com boom of the 1990s that
commercially revived the neighborhood. Remnants of old Belltown
include well-preserved facades.

DOWNTOWN SHOPPING SPREE

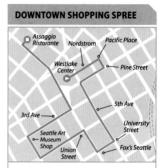

▶ **MID-MORNING**

Stop at **Westlake Center** *(see
p58)* and grab an espresso and
pastry at the stand in the plaza
before window-shopping in
Westlake's indoor mall. Inside,
Made in Washington offers a
large and creative inventory of
regionally produced merchandise. Walk across Pine Street
to find the spacious flagship
Nordstrom store *(see p58)*,
stocked with designer brands
and the absolute best of everything. Stop at Nike Seattle *(1500
6th Ave)*, where you can stock
up on the latest trends in sports-
wear, then move on to splurge
in **Pacific Place** mall *(see p59)*,
where customers can choose
from upscale stores including
Tiffany & Co., Coach, Kate Spade,
and J. Crew. Exit the mall on
Pine Street, turn right, and then
left on **5th Avenue** to **University
Street** for pricey boutiques
and fine jewelry, such as **Fox's
Seattle** *(405 University St)*.

Drop in for a quick cappuccino
and a bite to eat to refuel at one
of the many Starbucks shops,
then continue down University
Street to 1st Avenue and visit the
renowned **Seattle Art Museum
Shop** and its in-store art gallery,
where you can pick up striking
art prints and decorative objects.
Continue along 1st Avenue, heading north back to Pine Street, or,
if you're feeling hungry, walk a few
blocks northeast for an Italian
lunch at **Assaggio Ristorante**
(see p77) located on 4th Avenue.

See map on pp70–71 ←

Around Belltown

Performance at Moore Theatre

1 Moore Theatre
MAP J4 ■ 1932 2nd Ave ■ (206) 682-1414 ■ www.stgpresents.org

This historic theater stages theatrical productions, concerts, and lectures.

2 The Crocodile Back Bar
MAP H3 ■ 2505 1st Ave ■ (206) 441-4618 ■ www.thecrocodile.com

This live music venue showcases a variety of performers, including local bands. Good pizzas and drinks are served in a casual atmosphere.

3 Lenora Street Bridge
MAP H4

Leading from Western Avenue to the Elliott Bay piers, this elegant foot-bridge provides stellar views of West Seattle and the Olympic Mountains.

4 The Whisky Bar
MAP J4 ■ 2122 2nd Ave ■ www.thewhiskybar.com

This trendy bar in Belltown offers a large variety of whisky. It is good for pre-concert gatherings due to its proximity to the Moore Theatre.

5 Rendezvous/Jewel Box
MAP H3 ■ 2322 2nd Ave ■ www.therendezvous.rocks

Housing the Jewel Box Theater (see p53) built in 1926, this remod-eled bar attracts a hipster crowd.

6 Austin A. Bell Building
MAP H3 ■ 2326 1st Ave

Elmer Fisher, a noted commercial architect, designed this building in Gothic, Richardsonian, and Italianate styles. It houses condos and bars.

7 Sub Pop World Headquarters
MAP H3 ■ 2013 4th Ave ■ www.subpop.com

The local record label founded in the mid-1980s has its headquarters here. Sub Pop signed famous bands such as Nirvana and Soundgarden, putting Seattle on the rock music map.

8 Bathtub Gin & Co.
MAP J3 ■ 2205 2nd Ave ■ (206) 728-6069 ■ www.bathtubginseattle.com

A cozy spot in an old brick building, this intimate bar has been drawing fans of craft cocktails for years.

9 The Spheres and the Understory
MAP J4 ■ 2111 7th Ave ■ www.seattlespheres.com

These gigantic glass domes house the Amazon headquarters and an indoor botanic garden with more than 40,000 plants. Found beneath the Spheres is the Understory, a futuristic space that's home to many artists in residence.

10 Top Pot Doughnuts
MAP J3 ■ 2124 5th Ave ■ www.toppotdoughnuts.com

Grab a few doughnuts from this stylish café that offers house-roasted coffee and tasty homemade treats.

Top Pot Doughnuts' flagship store

Belltown Places to Shop

 Brick + Mortar
MAP J4 ■ 1210 4th Ave
(inside Fairmont Olympic Hotel)
■ (206) 588-2770 ■ www.brickmortar
seattle.com

This men's shoe boutique specializes in Alden shoes and is licensed to design and custom-make a limited collection. Service is impeccable.

 Vain
MAP J4 ■ 2018 1st Ave
■ (206) 441-3441 ■ www.vain.com

An innovative one-stop shop for hip consumers. Discover a full-service salon, an independent designer boutique, and an artists gallery.

3 **Patagonia**
MAP J4 ■ 2100 1st Ave ■ (206) 622-9700 ■ www.patagonia.com

The history of this purveyor of first-rate outdoor gear, rugged wear, and polar fleece comfort began with alpinist and founder Yvon Chouinard.

 Robbins Brothers, The Engagement Ring Store
MAP J4 ■ 2200 1st Ave ■ (206) 336-1456

It would be hard to miss this store with the arty neon sign of a bejeweled ring glowing above it. Staff are well informed and easy-going.

5 **Flora and Henri**
MAP K6 ■ 401 1st Ave S
■ (206) 749-9698 ■ www.flora
henri.com

This store sells handcrafted, upscale clothing and accessories for children, women, and men. It also has games and toys, small home decor items, and gifts.

6 **Kuhlman**
MAP J4 ■ 2419 1st Ave ■ (206) 453-6846 ■ www.kuhlmanseattle.com

Elegant clothing, including items from both heritage brands as well as smaller labels with new designers, is offered here. Kuhlman is well known for its bespoke tailoring.

7 **Endless Knot**
MAP H3 ■ 2300 1st Ave
■ (206) 448-0355

Stocking sizes small to large, this shop sells a range of artful, Asian-inspired designs.

Sell Your Sole Consignment Boutique

8 **Sell Your Sole Consignment Boutique**
MAP J4 ■ 2121 1st Ave, suite 101
■ (206) 443-2616 ■ www.sellyour
soleconsignment.com

Great service can be found at this women's clothing and shoes boutique, which stocks designer brands at up to 70 percent off their retail price. Look out for coveted labels such as McQueen, Chanel, Christian Louboutin, and Prada.

9 **Sassafras**
2307 1st Ave ■ (206) 420-7057
■ www.sassafras-seattle.com

Inventive and beautifully crafted clothing and jewelry in a changing array of styles, designed and made by local artists. Gracious sales staff.

10 **Singles Going Steady**
MAP J4 ■ 2219 2nd Ave
■ (206) 441-7396

A funky shop packed with pre-owned vinyl records and collectibles with a notable punk and indie vibe.

See map on pp70–71

Downtown Places to Shop

Colorful stationery and letterpress goods on display at Paper Hammer

1 Paper Hammer
MAP J4 ■ 1400 2nd Ave ■ (206) 682-3820 ■ www.paper-hammer.com

This quirky store sells letterpress arts and stationery, limited-run postcards, and notebooks.

2 Westlake Center
MAP K4 ■ 400 Pine St ■ (206) 467-1600

In addition to being a prime shopping destination, Westlake Center (see p58) hosts a range of exciting events and activities, such as free hobby classes.

3 Nordstrom
MAP K4 ■ 500 Pine St ■ (206) 628-2111

This top fashion retailer (see p58) stocks the very latest styles. Its much-awaited annual sales event around July and August is extremely popular.

4 Metsker Maps of Seattle
MAP J4 ■ 1511 1st Ave ■ (206) 623-8747 ■ www.metskers.com

Geography enthusiasts will lose themselves in this impressive store, where customers can peruse and buy a variety of maps, travel guides, moon charts, and globes.

5 Pendleton
MAP K4 ■ 1313 4th Ave ■ www.pendleton-usa.com

In 1863, British weaver Thomas Kay founded the Pendleton woolen company, which specializes in blankets and clothes for men and women.

6 Pacific Place
MAP K3 ■ 600 Pine St ■ (206) 405-2655

A five-floor haven (see p59) for shopaholics. There is also an incredible selection of eateries.

7 Fireworks
MAP K4 ■ Westlake Center, 400 Pine St ■ (206) 682-6462 ■ www. fireworksgallery.net

Shop here for handmade tableware, jewelry, clothing, whimsical books, and toys. There is a store at the airport, too, for that last-minute gift.

8 Isadoras Antique Jewelry
MAP J4 ■ 1601 1st Ave ■ (206) 441 7711 ■ www.isadoras.com

Offering new, designer, vintage, and private-label pieces, Isadora's collection of estate jewelry has been a hit since it opened in the late 1970s.

9 John Fluevog Shoes
MAP K4 ■ 205 Pine St ■ (206) 441-1065 ■ www.fluevog.com

High style and comfort are combined in John Fluevog's quirky yet affordable designs. The twice-yearly sales in January and July offer great value.

10 Mariners Team Store
MAP J4 ■ 1800 4th Ave ■ (206) 346-4327 ■ www.mlbshop.com

Buy official team jerseys and T-shirts, baseball caps, and other gift items emblazoned with the Mariners' logo.

Places to Eat

PRICE CATEGORIES

Price categories include a three-course meal for one, two glasses of wine, and all unavoidable extra charges including tax.

$ under $40 $$ $40–80 $$$ over $80

1 Cyclops
MAP H3 ▪ 2421 1st Ave
▪ (206) 441-1677 ▪ $

Interview and Details magazines have raved about this place, and local customers keep returning to enjoy a classic hummus plate.

2 Assaggio Ristorante
MAP J3 ▪ 2010 4th Ave ▪ (206) 441-1399 ▪ Closed Sun ▪ $$$

Savor tasty Italian cuisine such as *pappardelle cinghiale* (pasta ribbons with wild boar sauce) and *osso buco*. Many of the cheeses and produce items are imported from Italy.

3 Charlotte Restaurant & Lounge
MAP K5 ▪ 809 5th Ave ▪ (206) 496-0113 ▪ $$$

This restaurant offers fresh and seasonal Pacific Northwest seafood such as salmon, oysters, and halibut.

4 Queen City Grill
MAP J4 ▪ 2201 1st Ave
▪ (206) 402-5095 ▪ $$

One of the oldest bars in town, this place boasts a cozy and intimate atmosphere. The menu features scrumptious burgers and cocktails.

5 Radiator Whiskey
MAP J4 ▪ 94 Pike St, Pike Place Market ▪ (206) 467-4268 ▪ $$

Try the smoked and fried chicken with mac and cheese, and corn bread at this spot, known for Southern-style cooking.

6 Macrina Bakery & Café
MAP H3 ▪ 2408 1st Ave
▪ (206) 448-4032 ▪ Closed D ▪ $

A cherished bakery café famous for its bread pudding with fresh cream and berries, salads, and sandwiches.

7 Local 360
MAP H3 ▪ 2234 1st Ave
▪ (206) 441-9360 ▪ $

A community-minded restaurant that sources its ingredients from local farmers. Expect a casual, eclectic crowd.

8 Metropolitan Grill
MAP K5 ▪ 820 2nd Ave
▪ (206) 624-3287 ▪ $$$

Diners flock to this plush restaurant *(see p56)* for its custom dry-aged and succulently seasoned steaks. Its seafood dishes are excellent, too. Try the seafood sampler for the best fare.

Entrance to the Metropolitan Grill

9 The Pink Door
MAP J4 ▪ 1919 Post Alley, Pike Place Market ▪ (206) 443-3241 ▪ $$

Enjoy Italian-American classics, fresh local produce, and an extensive list of affordable wines here.

10 Belltown Pizza
MAP H3 ▪ 2422 1st Ave
▪ (206) 441-2653 ▪ $

With a neighborhood bar atmosphere, this pizzeria offers both standard and gourmet New-York style pizzas, which can be ordered by the slice. There is also a pasta selection. Try the gorgonzola-and-walnut-stuffed ravioli.

See map on pp70–71

TOP 10 Capitol Hill

Blanketing the long ridge that stretches northeast of downtown, Capitol Hill is the heart of Seattle's LGBTQ+ community and one of the coolest neighborhoods in the city. Abundant stores, music venues, clubs, restaurants, and cafés are peppered all along Broadway, Pike and Pine Streets, and 15th Avenue East, attracting people from all over the city. Key attractions found in this vibrant neighborhood include the vintage SIFF Cinema Egyptian, the expansive Elliott Bay Book Company, the Cornish College of the Arts, the Seattle Central College, and the Seattle Asian Art Museum in the sylvan setting of Volunteer Park.

Jimi Hendrix Statue

CAPITOL HILL

① **Top 10 Sights**
see pp79–81

① **Places to Eat**
see p85

① **Places to Shop**
see p83

① **LGBTQ+ Venues**
see p82

① **Cafés and Taverns**
see p84

Inside Unicorn Bar, Broadway

① Broadway

If it can be bought, it can be found on Broadway, the nerve center of Capitol Hill (see pp24–5). From East Pike to East Roy Streets, storefronts beckon consumers on the hunt for food, vintage and new clothing, vinyl records, and lots of coffee. On summer evenings, the density of pedestrian traffic along Broadway almost matches that of midtown Manhattan.

② East Capitol Hill
MAP E4

The area around 19th Avenue has its own restaurant scene – Hello Robin serves milk and carefully crafted cookies next to Molly Moon's Homemade Ice Cream take-out window. Cone & Steiner has a gourmet deli, and Fuel Coffee is a popular local hangout. There is a fountain plaza at Miller Community Center and its streets are lined with turn-of-the-century homes. A little farther north, there is cozy Volunteer Park Café.

③ Pike/Pine Corridor
MAP E4

Bisecting Capitol Hill are two of Seattle's busiest streets, offering their own flavor and subculture. You can find many of the area's LGBTQ+ venues on the blocks above and below Broadway, plus a great selection of taverns and stores that sell vintage housewares and furnishings. Although the city has tried to discourage their postings, you may notice colorful flyers stapled onto telephone poles and virtually any surface, advertising band concerts in the vicinity. If nothing else, they draw attention to the pulse that keeps this community thriving.

Posters on the Pike/Pine Corridor

4 Jimi Hendrix Statue

Daryl Smith, an artist once based at the former Fremont Fine Arts Foundry (now Fremont Foundry), created a life-sized bronze statue of Jimi Hendrix (see p25) that now graces the Pine Street sidewalk. It shows the musician in his trademark rockstar pose, kneeling in bell-bottoms with his Fender guitar pointed skyward. Before the Museum of Pop Culture was founded (see p38), inspired by Hendrix and his music, this installation was the best-known memorial dedicated to the guitarist.

5 Northwest Film Forum

MAP M3 ■ 1515 12th Ave ■ (206) 329-2629 ■ www.nwfilmforum.org

This festival screens more than 200 independent films every year in its two state-of-the-art modern theaters. The Forum is also host to events all year round, including talks by visiting directors and actors, and workshops for aspiring film-makers. It also acts as a venue for other festivals, such as the Translations Seattle Transgender film festival organized by the visionary collective, Three Dollar Bill Cinema.

Volunteer Park Water Tower

6 Volunteer Park Water Tower

MAP M1 ■ 1247 15th Ave E ■ (206) 684-4075 ■ Open 6am–11pm daily

Built by Seattle's water department in 1906, this 75-ft- (23-m-) tall brick tower with an observation deck was designed by the Olmsted Brothers. A short climb of 107 spiraling steps to the deck offers spectacular views of Puget Sound, the Space Needle, and the Olympic Mountains. Volunteer Park (see p44) is also the site of the Seattle Asian Art Museum (see p40) and the Volunteer Park Conservatory.

7 LGBTQ+ Scene

Capitol Hill is home to a wide variety of LGBTQ+ bars and clubs, as well as to Gay City: Seattle's LGBTQ Center (see p82).

8 Lake View Cemetery

MAP E3 ■ 1554 15th E ■ (206) 322-1582 ■ www.lakeview cemeteryassociation.com

Sitting on a hilltop past the northern end of Volunteer Park, this 1872-era cemetery is the final resting place for prominent Seattleites. Tombstones here identify important individuals in the city's history, whose names now grace present-day streets or area towns – Denny, Mercer, Boren, Maynard, Yesler, and Renton are a few examples. Lake View cemetery also draws the faithful fans of cinema star and martial arts master Bruce Lee (see p37) and his son, whose sculpted tombstones lie side by side.

SEATTLE PRIDE MARCH

What began as a protest in 1970 to commemorate the first anniversary of the Stonewall Riots in New York (which sparked the LGBTQ+ rights movement) has become a day of celebration, music, and pageantry. Although Capitol Hill can no longer accommodate the large numbers that come to participate – the rally (below) now takes place in Seattle Center – the Hill remains important for Seattle's LGBTQ+ community.

⑨ Neighborhood Homes

Stroll down the three-block stretch of Denny between Broadway and Olive Way to scout for charming Victorian and Craftsman-style homes and elegant balconies decorated with hanging flower baskets or offbeat art. Marvel at the opulent mansions on the blocks just south of Volunteer Park. Capitol Hill's adjacent Central District, south of Madison and north of 14th Avenue East, is a transitional neighborhood with gorgeous homes.

⑩ Cathedrals

St. Nicholas Russian Orthodox Cathedral: MAP M3; 1714 13th Ave
■ **St. Mark's Episcopal Cathedral: MAP E4; 1245 10th Ave E**

Capitol Hill has several landmark places of worship, such as the grand St. Mark's Episcopal Cathedral, which belongs to the Diocese of Olympia. Organ enthusiasts come from afar to play the 3,944-pipe Flentrop organ here. St. Nicholas Russian Orthodox Cathedral, one of the oldest parishes of the Russian Orthodox Church outside Russia, was established in 1930 by immigrants who fled the Russian Revolution in 1917. The structure's ornate turquoise *lukovitsa* (an "onion dome" style of cupolas from the 16th-century) and spires rise high above the trees and neighboring homes.

St. Mark's Episcopal Cathedral nave

EXPLORING PINE AND PIKE STREETS

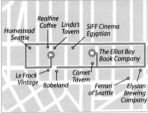

Realfine Coffee Linda's Tavern SIFF Cinema Egyptian Homestead Seattle The Elliot Bay Book Company Le Frock Vintage Babeland Comet Tavern Ferrari of Seattle Elysian Brewing Company

▶ MORNING

Begin your late morning walk at the corner of Pine and Boylston with a strong coffee at **Realfine Coffee** (616 E Pine St). Walk west towards the corner of Summit Avenue and East Pine Street and check out **Homestead Seattle** (501 E Pine St) for its beautiful antiques, then head to **Le Frock Vintage** (613 E Pike St) for its selection of vintage and new consignment clothing. One block north lies **Linda's Tavern** (see p84), a legendary local watering hole frequented by musicians and record label folk, which can be scoped out for a later visit. Cross Harvard Avenue and look out for the vintage **SIFF Cinema Egyptian** (see p53) on the right, which showcases independent and foreign films.

AFTERNOON

Cross Broadway, walk for four blocks, and turn right on 13th Avenue to Pike Street. Turn right and have lunch at **Elysian Brewing Company** (see p84), home of Seattle's most outstanding pale ale. Cross 12th Avenue and admire the gold-trimmed sports cars at **Ferrari of Seattle** (1401 12th Ave). Walk downhill on Pike to the **Comet Tavern** (see p84), a grungy place that is popular with local musicians and rock enthusiasts. Afterwards, stop by **Babeland** (see p82), a store selling various adult toys. Then grab a cup of coffee and a snack and lose yourself in the stacks of one of the city's most popular bookstores, **The Elliott Bay Book Company** (see p24).

See map on pp78–9

LGBTQ+ Venues

1 Union
MAP L3 ▪ 1009 E Union St ▪ (206) 328-1318 ▪ www.union seattle.com

Enjoy delicious bar food while watching music videos on the large-screen TVs at this welcoming spot. It has a heated, plant-filled outdoor patio and an indoor fireside lounge.

2 Re-bar
MAP L3 ▪ 1114 Howell St ▪ www.rebarseattle.com

This dive bar has high-spirited live acts on stage, including some of the area's best DJs. The entrance sign sums up its philosophy, "no minors, drunks, drugs, bigots, or loudmouths."

Gay City, an LGBTQ+ center

3 Gay City: Seattle's LGBTQ+ Center
MAP L3 ▪ 517 E Pike St ▪ (206) 860-6969 ▪ www.gaycity.org

Featuring a library and a resource center, this organization offers health services, events, and art shows which promote wellness in the community.

4 Babeland
MAP L3 ▪ 707 E Pike St ▪ (206) 328-2914

Primarily a store selling sex toys, this spot also sponsors sex work-shops that both amuse and shock.

5 The Crescent Lounge
MAP L3 ▪ 1413 E Olive Way ▪ (206) 565-8827

This local dive bar is a trendy hipster hangout with entertaining karaoke and reasonably priced drinks.

6 C C Attle's
MAP L2 ▪ 1701 E Olive Way ▪ (206) 726-0565 ▪ www.ccattles.net

Locals come here before hitting the dance spots. Expect friendly bartenders, well-priced drinks, and a good variety of music. There are darts and pool tables, too.

7 Eagle
MAP L3 ▪ 314 E Pike St ▪ www.seattleeagle.com

Seattle's oldest leather bar, Eagle has a lively atmosphere that attracts a crowd driven by studs, black leather straps, and hard rock music.

8 The Cuff Complex
MAP M3 ▪ 1533 13th Ave ▪ www.cuffcomplex.com

An exclusive gay men's bar and dance complex catering to a mixed crowd. Arrive on Sundays for a kegger blowout.

9 Diesel Seattle
MAP M3 ▪ 1413 14th Ave ▪ (206) 322-1080

Visitors can expect a fun and friendly crowd (and plenty of leather) at one of the city's oldest gay bars. Drinks are generous and bar food plentiful. Taco Tuesdays are hugely popular.

10 Wildrose
MAP M3 ▪ 1021 E Pike St ▪ www.thewildrosebar.com

One of the oldest lesbian bars on the West Coast, Wildrose does not encourage many solo male guests. However, a number of couples do visit the club for the dancing, strong drinks, karaoke, open mike nights, poetry readings, and pool games.

Places to Shop

Racks of colorful second-hand clothes for sale at Pretty Parlor

 Pretty Parlor
MAP L2 ▪ 119 Summit Ave E
▪ (206) 405-2883 ▪ www.pretty
parlor.com
Stocked full with vintage and indie clothing for women, this store is the place to find a unique wardrobe item.

2 Martin-Zambito Gallery
MAP L4 ▪ 1117 Minor Ave
▪ (206) 726-9509
Established in 1986, this art gallery specializes in 19th- to 21st-century American and early Northwest Regionalism, with special emphasis put on contemporary figurative art, and early women artists.

3 Fleet Feet Sports
MAP L3 ▪ 911 E Pine St
▪ www.fleetfeetseattle.com
This store stocks dozens of top brands. The knowledgeable staff can fit even the most finicky sports lovers with proper accessories.

4 The Elliott Bay Book Company
Peruse the huge selection at this excellent independent bookstore and Seattle institution (see p24). It also has its own café, Little Oddfellows.

5 Sugar Pill Apothecary
MAP M3 ▪ 900 E Pine St ▪ (206) 322-7455 ▪ www.sugarpillseattle.com
Much of the inventory at this quirky store is produced by women-owned businesses. Organic chocolates, spa goods, and spices are some of the items sold here.

6 Wall of Sound
MAP L3 ▪ 1205 E Pike St
▪ www.wosound.com
A treasured shop selling new and rare CDs and LPs, Wall of Sound carries obscure recordings of rock, jazz, electronic, modern classical, and other unusual tracks.

7 Melrose Market
MAP L2 ▪ 1531 Melrose Ave
▪ www.melrosemarketseattle.com
Some of Seattle's best retailers and independent food purveyors are featured at this indoor market (see p59) Try tapas at Terra Plata or an organic sandwich from Homegrown.

8 Cone & Steiner
MAP F4 ▪ 532 19th Ave E ▪ (206) 582-1928 ▪ www.coneandsteiner.com
This gourmet neighborhood market has wine and chocolate tastings and a top-quality take-out deli.

9 Quest Bookshop
MAP L3 ▪ 717 Broadway
Ave E ▪ (206) 323-4281 ▪ www.
questbooks.com
In addition to more than 11,000 titles covering religion, mysticism, and spirituality, Quest offers personal astrological charts and tarot decks.

10 Retail Therapy
MAP M3 ▪ 905 E Pike St
▪ (206) 324-4092 ▪ www.ineed
retailtherapy.com
This store sells clothing, accessories, jewelry, fragrances, gifts, and art by independent artists and designers.

See map on pp78–9

Cafés and Taverns

Exposed brickwork and trendy lighting in Victrola Coffee Roasters

 Victrola Coffee Roasters
MAP E4 ▪ 411 15th Ave E
▪ www.victrolacoffee.com ▪ $

A real neighborhood café that prides itself on roasting its coffee in-house, using beans from small farms.

2 Caffè Vita
MAP M3 ▪ 1005 E Pike St
▪ (206) 712-2132 ▪ $

Dark walls and ceilings, wooden floors, and excellent coffee set the tone here. It roasts its own coffee; look through the back window to see the apparatus.

3 Tavern Law
MAP M3 ▪ 1406 12th Ave
▪ (206) 322-9734 ▪ $

A speakeasy-style lounge offering well-made cocktails and comfort fare to those looking to unwind.

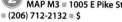 **4 Chop Suey**
MAP E4 ▪ 1325 E Madison St
▪ (206) 538-0556 ▪ $

Locals flock to this place *(see p54)* for the hip-hop acts on Sundays and hard rock bands the rest of the week.

5 Linda's Tavern
MAP L3 ▪ 707 E Pine St
▪ (206) 325-1220 ▪ $

Linda Derschang, a local business owner, created a hip bar for locals in 1994 (who tended to be rock stars). Drinks and decent food are on offer.

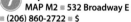 **6 Hopvine Pub**
MAP E4 ▪ 507 15th Ave E
▪ (206) 328-3120 ▪ $

This neighborhood bar serves tasty pub fare and good handcrafted cask ales from small breweries.

 7 Espresso Vivace
MAP M2 ▪ 532 Broadway E
▪ (206) 860-2722 ▪ $

Popular for its striking latte art and slow-roasted blends, this café also offers a great selection of pastries. There is a children's play area on site.

8 Comet Tavern
MAP M3 ▪ 922 E Pike St ▪ $

A legendary hangout for rockers and great pretenders alike. This is just a normal tavern with some pool tables, but the crowd tells a different tale.

 9 Fuel Coffee
MAP F4 ▪ 610 19th Ave E
▪ (206) 329-4700 ▪ www.fuelcoffee
seattle.com ▪ $

This cozy café serves strong espresso along with treats from local bakeries. The walls display work by local artists.

10 Elysian Brewing Company
MAP M3 ▪ 1221 E Pike St ▪ (206) 906-9148 ▪ $

The food here *(see p55)* rates among some of the best pub grub in town.

Places to Eat

PRICE CATEGORIES
Price categories include a three-course meal for one, two glasses of wine, and all unavoidable extra charges including tax.

$ under $40 $$ $40–80 $$$ over $80

1 Rancho Bravo Tacos
MAP M4 ▪ 1001 E Pine St
▪ (206) 322-9399 ▪ $

A colorful, no-frills taqueria, with friendly, attentive staff. Loyal customers love the affordable plates of fresh Mexican fare.

2 DeLuxe Bar & Grill
MAP M1 ▪ 625 Broadway E
▪ (206) 324-9697 ▪ $

Serves an enviable list of brews and better-than-usual pub fare including nachos, burgers, and salads.

3 Witness
MAP M1 ▪ 410 Broadway E
▪ (206) 329-0248 ▪ Closed Mon–Fri L, Sat & Sun D ▪ $$

Enjoy Southern-style food, paired with craft cocktails and beers, in a bar setting with church pews for seating.

4 Honey Hole
MAP L3 ▪ 703 E Pike St
▪ (206) 709-1399 ▪ $

Find your way to this heartwarming source of Capitol Hill's biggest and most succulent sandwiches.

5 Garage
MAP M4 ▪ 1130 Broadway ▪ (206) 322-2296 ▪ $

A crowded, over-21 spot for pool, bowling, laser tag, and casual food.

Garage diner

6 Terra Plata
MAP L3 ▪ 1501 Melrose Ave
▪ (206) 325-1501 ▪ $$$

Enjoy bistro-style plates at this restaurant that focuses on local produce. Its rooftop patio is the place to be.

7 Lark
MAP M4 ▪ 952 E Seneca St
▪ (206) 323-5275 ▪ www.larkseattle. com ▪ $$

An upscale bistro *(see p56)* with big sharing plates of Northwest cuisine.

8 Annapurna Café
MAP M3 ▪ 1833 Broadway
▪ (206) 320-7770 ▪ $

This restaurant offers dishes from countries such as Nepal and India. Choose from dumplings, tandoori dishes, or curry items. There is no wheelchair access here.

9 Via Tribunali
MAP L3 ▪ 913 E Pike St
▪ (206) 322-9234 ▪ $$

Some of the best Italian pizza in town, with generous, delicious toppings and excellent crusts.

10 Quinn's Pub
MAP L3 ▪ 1001 E Pike St
▪ (206) 325-7711 ▪ $

A popular, upscale bar where guests dine on gourmet burgers and modern American comfort fare. The wild boar Sloppy Joe and foie gras poutine are delicious.

🔟 Fremont

Fremont declared itself an "artists' republic" in the 1960s, when a community of students, artists, and bohemians moved in, attracted by low rents. The name reflects the unflagging spirit of independence, eccentricity, and nonconformity here. In retrospect, what may have begun as an idealistic artists' enclave was more accurately an early sign of gentrification. The scenic Lake Washington Ship Canal and part of Lake Union create its southern border, and passing boats continually refresh the view. The drawbridge on busy Fremont Avenue rises and falls many times a day, and heavy traffic backs up the hill. The quaint neighborhood spawns new boutiques, clubs, and restaurants that keep changing the identity of this area. As Seattle grows, more people seek homes here, only minutes away from downtown.

Art Nouveau lamp, Fremont Market

FREMONT

Top 10 Sights
see pp89–91

Places to Eat
see p95

Places to Shop
see p94

Burke-Gilman Trail Features
see p93

Fremont Culture
see p92

Previous pages Skyscrapers lining Bell Harbor Marina on the Seattle Waterfront

① Lenin Statue

MAP D2 ▪ 3526 Fremont Ave N

Slovakian sculptor Emil Venkov (1937–2017) found little interest in his 7-ton (6,350-kg), 16-ft- (5-m-) tall likeness of Russian revolutionary Vladimir Lenin after the collapse of the Soviet Union. A visiting American, Lewis Carpenter, paid $13,000 for the work and had it shipped via the Panama Canal to his hometown near Seattle. After Carpenter died in 1994, artist and Fremont Foundry owner Peter Bevis managed to have the bronze Lenin statue installed in this neighborhood.

② Fremont Troll

MAP D2 ▪ Intersection of Aurora Ave (Hwy 99) & N 36th St

An icon of Fremont's free spirit is a 18-ft- (5.5-m-) tall troll created by

Fremont Troll under Aurora Bridge

Steve Badanes, Will Martin, Donna Walter, and Ross Whitehead, after a national competition sponsored by the Fremont Arts Council (see p92). In 1989, the council decided that public art was the best use for a dark space underneath a highway bridge. Made from wire, steel, and concrete, with one shiny metal eye, this giant sculpture seems to crawl out from underneath the bridge, while at the same time squashing a Volkswagen Beetle in his left hand. The troll's location under the north end of Aurora Bridge means that it features on almost every tour.

③ Fremont Bridge

MAP D3 ▪ 3020 Westlake Ave N

The lowest of four bridges built over the Lake Washington Ship Canal, Fremont Bridge connects Fremont to Queen Anne and two main arterials to downtown. Due to the bridge's low clearance, it faces frequent openings from passing vessels. Neon art adorns a portion of the span, depicting Rapunzel with her blonde hair cascading from a tower's window.

Fremont Bridge

NORTH 36TH STREET

NORTH 35TH STREET

NORTH 34TH STREET

Burke-Gilman Trail

N Northlake Way

FREMONT PLACE N

EVANSTON AVE NORTH

FREMONT AVE NORTH

NORTH 36TH ST

0 meters 150
0 yards 150

INTERLAKE AVE N

ASHWORTH AVE N

WOODLAWN AVENUE N

DENSMORE AVE N

WALLINGFORD AVE N

BURKE AVE N

MERIDIAN AVENUE NORTH

BAGLEY AVENUE NORTH

CORLISS AVE NORTH

NORTH PACIFIC ST

N NORTHLAKE WAY

N 36TH ST

N 35TH ST

NORTH 34TH ST

N NORTHLAKE WAY

Gas Works Park

Burke-Gilman Trail

Lake Union

0 meters 300
0 yards 300

4 Sunday Street Market
MAP D2 ■ N 34th St ■ (206) 781-6776 ■ Open 10am–4pm Sun ■ www.fremontmarket.com

The Fremont Sunday Market has withstood the test of time, real estate development, and even lawsuits from neighboring businesses. Begun in 1990 to foster a pedestrian-friendly community and provide an outlet for artists and independent vendors to sell their wares, the market hosts up to 200 booths of crafts, imported goods, furniture, food, and knick-knacks that defy description.

5 Dinosaur Topiaries
MAP D2 ■ Intersection of Phinney Ave N & N 34th St

Two ivy-covered dinosaur topiaries, which had formerly decorated the lawn near the Pacific Science Center (see p15) at Seattle Center, now grace the neighborhood's narrow Fremont Canal Park. To save them from being razed, History House and a group of Fremont artists purchased them in 1999 for $1. The young *apatosauri* and its 66-ft- (20-m-) long mother are now sanctioned by the city and fully integrated into a neighborhood-wide sculpture garden.

6 Fremont Canal Park
MAP C2 ■ Phinney Ave N & 2nd Ave NW ■ (206) 684-4075

A lovely landscaped strip, not a great deal wider than a stretch

Waterfront path, Fremont Canal Park

of the Burke-Gilman Trail (see p93), attracts tourists all year round. The park creates scenic viewpoints along the canal and offers several places to sit, play chess, enjoy a picnic, and watch the world go by. Pedestrians do not need to dodge speeding bicycles, since there is a separate path here for cyclists.

7 Waiting for the Interurban
MAP D2 ■ N 34th St & Fremont Ave N

Frozen in time, artist Richard Beyer's celebrated cast aluminum sculpture, lies at Fremont's busiest road intersection, where a community trolley once stopped. It depicts six human forms with grim expressions standing side by side, and a dog with a human face. Legend has it that the dog bears the face of the activist Arman Napoleon Stepanian, who sparked the recycling movement some 30 years ago. The work pokes fun at modern humanity's ennui, and is among the city's earliest public art installations.

Waiting for the Interurban **sculpture**

8 Fremont Ferry and Sunday Ice Cream Cruise

MAP D3 ▪ (206) 713-8446
▪ Sunday Ice Cream Cruise: 11am–5pm Sun ▪ Adm ▪ www.seattlewatertours.com

A labor of love for Captain Larry Kezner, this passenger-only ferry plies the waters of Lake Union from the north shore in Fremont to Lake Union Park on the south shore in the summer. For a more regular boat service, the Sunday Ice Cream Cruise departs every Sunday on the hour from Lake Union Park.

9 Fremont Brewing Company

MAP D2 ▪ 1050 N 34th St ▪ (206) 420-2407 ▪ www.fremontbrewing.com

This kid and dog-friendly "urban beer garden" has become a neighborhood hub for all ages. It specialises in microbrews made with local ingredients, and in promoting community causes and events.

Entrance to the History House

10 History House

MAP D2 ▪ 900 N 34th St
▪ (206) 675-8875 ▪ Adm (donation)
▪ www.historyhouse.org

Seattle's colorful past can be viewed at History House, where a dedicated group of historians help preserve the heritage of the city's distinct neighborhoods. A three-sided sepia-tone wall mural depicts over 100 years of Seattle's history in the arts, technology, and industry. Visitors can browse the carefully curated rotating displays of various neighborhoods in Seattle. Other features here include a gift shop and a sculpture garden.

A MORNING AROUND FREMONT

▶ MORNING

Start the day with an espresso at **Espresso To Go** *(3512 Fremont Place N)*. Take the crosswalk just outside the door to N 35th Street, turning right to view the neon-adorned Army surplus missile known as **The Rocket** *(see p93)*. Turn left on Evanston and walk a block to **PCC Community Markets** *(600 N 34th St)*, an organic food market, to pick up a delicious carry-out lunch.

Turn left on Evanston for an unobstructed view of the **Fremont Cut** and **Fremont Bridge** *(see p89)*. Turn right along the Canal path, walk about a block until you see the **Dinosaur Topiaries** at the entrance to the **Fremont Canal Park** – a great place to enjoy a waterfront picnic. The **Old Trolley Barn** *(see p93)* is a historic brick building that now houses **Theo Chocolate** *(see p92)*, a gourmet chocolate factory. Enjoy the walk down the canal path, spotting sailboats or kayakers. When turning back, exit the park at the topiaries and continue along N 34th Street. During the Sunday Street Market, there are blocks of vendors here. Continue three blocks to Fremont Avenue N, by the Fremont Bridge, passing the sculpture, *Waiting for the Interurban*, on a traffic island across the street. Turn left on Fremont Avenue N, and admire the **Center of the Universe signpost**, which is a half-block later on another traffic island where Fremont Place begins. Stop at **Simply Desserts** *(3421 Fremont Ave N)* for indulging in some of the richest treats in town.

See map on pp88–9 ←

Fremont Culture

Parade performers, Fremont Fair

1 Fremont Fair

The Solstice Parade *(see p62)*, which includes colorfully clad participants, people-powered floats, and even naked cyclists, kicks off this fair with food, crafts, and music.

2 First Fridays Art Walk

Fremont Foundry: MAP C2; 154 N 35th

On the first Friday of each month, galleries organize self-guided art walks to local studios and establishments, including the Fremont Foundry and the Fremont Coffee Company *(see p57)*.

3 Trolloween

MAP D2 ■ 36th St N under Aurora Ave

A lively parade that begins its route near the Fremont Troll *(see p89)*, this takeoff on Halloween ends at a bizarre masked ball with light shows and live entertainment.

4 Theo Chocolate

MAP D2 ■ 3400 Phinney Ave N ■ (206) 632-5100 ■ www.theo chocolate.com

Visitors can see chocolate being made and can feast on samples at the country's first organic, fair trade chocolate company. It sources its beans from all over the world.

5 The Backdoor at Roxy's

MAP C2 ■ 462 N 36th St ■ (206) 632-7322 ■ www.backdooratroxys.com

This speakeasy lounge has an edgy, Baroque-style decor. Go for the Ryan Gosling cocktail and Fremont fries.

6 Fremont Arts Council

MAP D2 ■ 3940 Fremont Ave N ■ (206) 547-7440 ■ www. fremontartscouncil.org

Based in an elementary school's 1892-vintage powerhouse, this community organization supports artists and creative expression.

7 Glass Art

Edge of Glass: MAP D2; 513 N 36th St; (206) 632-7807; www.edgeofglass.com

Local artist Dale Chihuly's *(see p41)* influence can be seen in Seattle's glass studios such as Edge of Glass.

8 Moisture Festival

MAP C2 ■ 4301 Leary Way NW ■ www.moisturefestival.org

This addition to the funky Fremont scene combines elements of burlesque and carnival for four weeks in spring. It is held at the old Hale's Ales Brewery.

9 Pumpkin-Carving Contests

www.fremontoktober fest.com

During the Oktoberfest celebrations – Fremont's beer festival – hilarious chainsaw pumpkin-carving competitions take place on the stage.

Lily Verlaine, Moisture Festival

10 Fremont Library

MAP D2 ■ 731 N 35th St ■ (206) 684-4084

The city's most charming library attracts resident literati who spend hours here. It also has free public computers and Wi-Fi.

Burke-Gilman Trail Features

 Lake Washington Rowing Club
MAP D3 ■ 910 N Northlake Way

Both the local athletic teams and amateur rowers hoist their boats into the river from here. The club's nonprofit activities also include training lessons for beginners.

 Old Trolley Barn
MAP D2 ■ N 34th & Phinney Ave N

A brick warehouse, this barn was once home to Seattle's early mass transit vehicles – the trolleys. Since then, the building has been, among other things, a microbrewery, and now houses the Theo Chocolate store.

3 Dock Overlook
MAP C2

Situated right on the water, this fenced-in area with benches and a roof is ideal for watching birds, boats and sunsets. It affords superb views of Salmon Bay's dry-dock industry and the vast Olympic Mountains.

 The Rocket
MAP D2 ■ N 35th & Evanston Ave N

When an Army surplus store closed in Belltown, its outside adornment ended up in the hands of a group of Fremont sculptors and painters who renovated the World War II-era missile and placed it here, atop the Burnt Sugar shoe store.

The Rocket

 Bridges

The Burke-Gilman Trail makes its way under the Fremont Bridge (see p89) and the Aurora Bridge. Both span the Ship Canal, although only the drawbridge opens for boat traffic.

Fremont Bridge, opened for boats

 Rope Swing
MAP D2

Sunny summer days attract a crowd of rope-swingers who get dunked in the canal near Phinney Ave N.

 Adobe Systems
MAP D3 ■ 801 N 34th St
■ (206) 675-7000

This software company's building was designed to resemble Fremont's erstwhile industrial structures.

8 Indoor Sun Shoppe
MAP C2 ■ 160 N Canal St

Huge plants decorate the shopfront of Seattle's favorite neighborhood home and garden store.

9 Fremont Mischief
MAP C2 ■ 132 N Canal St
■ www.fremontmischief.com

This distillery and shop offers tours and tastings of spirits made on site, such as gin, vodka, and rye whisky.

10 Gravel Plant
MAP C2

The mounds of gravel and asphalt here create a stark contrast to the serenity of the parkland nearby.

See map on pp88–9

Places to Shop

Browsing vinyls at Jive Time Records

1 Jive Time Records
MAP D2 ▪ 3506 Fremont Ave N ▪ (206) 632-5483 ▪ www.jivetime records.com

Discover quality vintage jazz, hip-hop, and electronic albums – no music obsessions are too obscure here, and there are heaps of vinyls to be found.

2 Dusty Strings
MAP D2 ▪ 3406 Fremont Ave N ▪ (206) 634-1662 ▪ www. dustystrings.com

Since 1979, this store has attracted players and fans of folk music looking for a levered harp, fiddle, acoustic guitar, or a workshop on dulcimers.

3 evo
MAP D2 ▪ 3500 Stone Way N ▪ (206) 973-4470 ▪ www.evo.com

Find an array of outdoor gear ranging from skis to skateboards at this huge sporting goods store. It is located in the Fremont Collective, which is also home to the city's only indoor skate-park – All Together Skatepark (ATS).

4 Bellefleur Lingerie Boutique
MAP D2 ▪ 3504 Fremont Pl N ▪ (206) 545-0222 ▪ www.bellefleur lingerie.com

This chic lingerie boutique caters to brides and anyone else who wishes to indulge in some luxury. Sleepwear and lounge apparel can also be found.

5 Les Amis
MAP D2 ▪ 3420 Evanston Ave N ▪ (206) 632-2877 ▪ www. lesamis-inc.com

Window-shoppers find it hard to resist the rustic charm of this lovely women's boutique that stocks designer clothing and jewelry sourced from around the globe.

6 Frame Up Studios
MAP D2 ▪ 3515 Fremont Ave N ▪ (206) 547-4657 ▪ www.frame upstudios.com

A simple framing shop that turned itself into a lovely and sophisticated resource for one-of-a-kind gift items.

7 Show Pony
MAP D2 ▪ 3501 Fremont Ave N ▪ (206) 706-4188 ▪ www.showpony boutique.com

This well-curated boutique stocks vintage consignment fashions, clothing, jewelry, and accessories.

8 Ophelia's Books
MAP C2 ▪ 3504 Fremont Ave N ▪ (206) 632-3759 ▪ www. opheliasbooks.com

There are three floors of new and used books here, with a large selection of rare and out-of-print editions.

9 Fremont Vintage Mall
MAP D2 ▪ 3419 Fremont Place N ▪ (206) 329-4460 ▪ www.fremont vintagemall.com

This underground warren features vintage clothing, furniture, and records, among other treasures.

10 Essenza Inc
MAP D2 ▪ 615 N 35th St ▪ (206) 547-4895 ▪ www.essenza-inc.com

A funky shop, Essenza Inc sells a well-chosen assortment of cosmetics, perfumes, bath and skincare products, jewelry, and lingerie.

➤ *See map on pp88–9*

Places to Eat

PRICE CATEGORIES
Price categories include a three-course
meal for one, two glasses of wine, and all
unavoidable extra charges including tax.

$ under $40 $$ $40–80 $$$ over $80

1 Revel
MAP D2 ▪ 403 N 36th S
▪ (206) 547-2040 ▪ Closed Sun ▪ $$

Tuck into Korean fusion cuisine in
this casual space with its pleasant
outdoor patio. The rice bowls, ramen,
and *soju* (rice liquor) served in the
adjoining bar are especially good.

2 Kwanjai Thai Cuisine
MAP D2 ▪ 469 N 36th St
▪ (206) 632-3656 ▪ $

It is hard to go wrong when ordering
off the specials board or the regular
menu in this Thai restaurant.

3 Canlis
MAP D3 ▪ 2576 Aurora Ave N
▪ (206) 283-3313 ▪ $$$

Housed in a 1950s building, Canlis
(see p56) epitomizes fine dining. The
sweeping views of the city from here
are an added delight. Dress to impress
for an unforgettable experience.

4 Joule
MAP D2 ▪ 3506 Stone Way N
▪ (206) 632-5685 ▪ $$

A Korean fusion restaurant, Joule is
popular across town for its themed
brunch buffet. The eclectic, mouth-
watering dishes created by talented
chefs have won the res-
taurant critical acclaim.

5 Paseo

MAP D2
▪ 4225 Fremont Ave N
▪ (206) 545-7440
▪ Closed Mon ▪ $

This busy restaurant
churns out some of the
most lauded sandwiches
in Seattle. The most
popular are Caribbean
Roast and Paseo Press.

6 Hale's Ales Brewery
MAP C2 ▪ 4301 Leary Way NW
▪ (206) 782-0737 ▪ $

Customers sip on the latest
concoctions brewed in one of the
city's first brewpubs *(see p55)*.

7 Cafe Turko
MAP D2 ▪ 750 N 34th St
▪ (206) 284-9954 ▪ $

This family-owned spot offers
an extensive menu of Turkish
specialties, including hummus,
pide, dolmas, mezzes, and kebabs.
There are multiple vegan options.

8 Uneeda Burger
MAP D2 ▪ 4302 Fremont Ave N
▪ (206) 547-2600 ▪ $$

A friendly restaurant serving tasty
burgers and sides. Also on offer are
milkshakes and a selection of beers.

9 Local Tide
MAP D2 ▪ 401 N 36th St
▪ (206) 420-4685 ▪ $

Local vendors offer huge sandwiches
filled with fresh seafood at this
small, industrial-style space.

10 El Camino
MAP D2 ▪ 607 N 35th St
▪ (206) 632-7303 ▪ $$

This is the place for great Mexican
dishes using ingredients such as
duck, pork, shrimp, fish, and chipotle
peppers. Don't miss the margaritas.

Elegant decor at El Camino

🔟 Ballard

In the late 19th century, Scandinavian loggers and fishermen established a working waterfront, which is still functioning today. Seattle annexed Ballard in 1907, taking advantage of the huge economic growth the mill town fostered; by then Ballard was the state's third largest city. The late 1990s dot-com boom made real estate prices skyrocket, and led to the opening of new boutiques, art galleries, and restaurants. Popular tourist attractions include the Hiram M. Chittenden Locks and Golden Gardens. The National Nordic Museum celebrates the culture of the area's Scandinavian Americans, and every May 17, the Norwegian Constitution Day Parade takes over the streets.

Moorings at Fishermen's Terminal

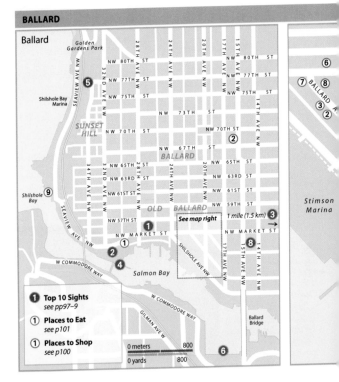

BALLARD

1 Top 10 Sights
see pp97–9

① Places to Eat
see p101

① Places to Shop
see p100

0 meters 800
0 yards 800

Clogs in the National Nordic Museum

1 National Nordic Museum

MAP B1 ■ 2655 NW Market St
■ Open 10am–5pm Tue–Sun (to 8pm
Thu) ■ Adm ■ www.nordicmuseum.org

With rooms organized by country,
this museum illustrates the history
of Scandinavian immigration to
the Pacific Northwest. Founded in
1980, it is the only museum in the
United States to revere the legacy
of immigrants from the five Nordic
countries – Finland, Iceland, Norway,
Denmark, and Sweden. Visitors are
enlightened by rotating and permanent exhibits, including colorful
Old World textiles, rare china, books
and bibles, woodworking tools, and
carved wooden ale bowls. There is
also an extensive music library.

2 Carl S. English Jr. Botanical Gardens

MAP B1 ■ 3015 NW 54th St ■ (206)
783-7059 ■ Open 7am–9pm Wed–
Mon, 7am–6pm Tue

Take a little time for a delightful
promenade through the greenery
of lush trees and rare plants that
fill the garden's 7 acres (3 ha),
bordering the locks on the northern
side of the Ship Canal. The gift shop,
which also serves visitors to the
locks, offers a guide to help
visitors identify the plants.

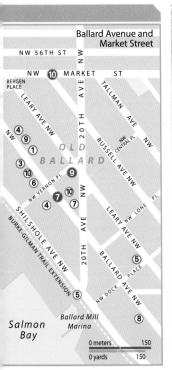

Ballard Avenue and Market Street

Verdant borders, Botanical Gardens

3 Woodland Park Zoo

MAP D1 ■ 5500 Phinney Ave
N ■ (206) 548-2500 ■ Open May–Sep:
9:30am–6pm daily; Oct–Apr: 9:30am–
4pm daily ■ Adm ■ www.zoo.org

Spread across a large forested tract
just east of Ballard, this zoo is known
for its conservation efforts. It is home
to more than 300 animal species,
most of which are housed in spacious
environments that have been built
to replicate their natural habitats.
Visitors can wander along the tidy
paths, learn more about the animals
from the zoo-keepers, or even go
on a vintage carousel ride.

4 Ballard Locks

Every year, 100,000 vessels pass through the Ship Canal's Hiram M. Chittenden Locks *(see pp26–7)*, and nearly as many tourists come to marvel at the site between Salmon Bay and Shilshole Bay. Named after a retired US Army Corps of Engineers general, the locks are the result of sophisticated engineering, and the sheer variety of pleasure boats and industrial ships that are able to pass through impress visitors. The locks also feature fish ladders to allow migrating salmon to leave from or return to their home streams, which is best observed between June and September. Do not miss the small but fascinating visitors' center, with its informative short film and displays.

A boat emerging from a lock

5 Golden Gardens

MAP P2 ▪ 8498 Seaview Pl NW ▪ (206) 684-4075

Ballard's largest park *(see p45)* offers an expanse of forested trails, beaches, picnic areas, and views of the Olympic Mountains and Puget Sound. Originally, the gardens stood at the end of the line for streetcars, which were funded by realtors who wanted residents to get away from the city. Cool summer nights bring large groups to huddle around bonfires, while sunny days see hundreds playing volleyball and getting tans. There is also a dog area, and a boat ramp at the marina.

Golden Gardens waterfront

6 Fishermen's Terminal

MAP C2 ▪ 3919 18th Ave W

The terminal provides moorage for more than 700 commercial fishing vessels and workboats. Because of the sheltered port and the area's industries and businesses, many Northwest commercial fishermen regard Seattle as the best center for maintenance and repair. The Fishermen's Memorial sculpture, crafted from bronze-and-stone is inscribed with the names of more than 670 local men and women, and commemorates lives lost to commercial fishing since 1900. There are two seafood restaurants located here – one is a take-out with dockside tables.

7 Ballard Avenue

MAP B1

From the roaring 1890s through the Great Depression, the four-block stretch of brick-paved Ballard Avenue defined the *raison d'être* of a mill town that also had a thriving boatbuilding and fishing industry. The 19th-century architecture is stunning, and it is easy to imagine a street filled with timber millworkers, fishermen, fishmongers, as well as the banks, saloons, and bordellos that served them. In 1976, Sweden's King Carl XVI Gustaf read the proclamation that listed Ballard Avenue on the Register of Historic Places.

8 Bardahl Sign

MAP C1

Whether traveling on foot or via bicycle, car, bus, boat, or plane, the towering, red neon advertisement for Bardahl automotive oil treatment is unmissable. The sign's ascending flashes harken back to Ballard's industrial roots, and to the company founder Ole Bardahl, Ballard resident and Norwegian immigrant. The sign is one of Seattle's favorite landmarks.

Sunday Farmers' Market entrance

⑨ Sunday Farmers' Market
MAP B2 ■ Open 10am–3pm

Like many neighborhoods in Seattle, Ballard attracts weekend shoppers by organizing for regional farmers, artists, and craftspeople to fill the closed-off streets around Ballard Avenue with an Old World market. The market operates year-round, but when summer is in full swing, growers from the arid east side of the Cascade Mountains bring their bounty of organic produce.

⑩ Market Street
MAP B1

The nerve center of Ballard has a vast selection of Scandinavian gift shops, stores, cafés, and taverns lining both sides of the street. The street's melange of local businesses and creative signage reflects the community's small-town character that has remained intact since the days before Ballard officially became part of Seattle.

A MORNING WALK DOWN BALLARD AVENUE

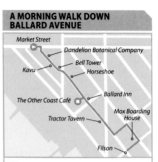

▶ MORNING

Begin at the terminus of Ballard Avenue at **Market Street**. Walk down the west side of the street. Check out the gear at **Kavu** *(5419 Ballard Ave NW)*, an independent retailer of outdoor wear that is appropriate for everything from walking in woodland to dining out. Crossing the street, head to the **Dandelion Botanical Company** *(see p100)* for natural apothecary items. At the point where 22nd Avenue meets Ballard Avenue stands the large, brick **Bell Tower**, rebuilt from the original after the City Hall tower was destroyed by the 1965 earthquake. Next, walk over to the enticing and luxurious **Horseshoe** boutique *(see p100)* featuring local and international designer clothing and makeup. At the following intersection, stop to notice the stylized roof crest of the **Ballard Inn** *(5300 Ballard Ave NW)*, which still has a "Bank Building" sign from its previous occupier over a century ago.

Cross the street and look out for **Tractor Tavern** *(see p55)*, a musical outlet for local as well as touring musicians who play country rock and jazz. Find exclusive and signature items at **Filson** *(5101 Ballard Ave NW)*, an outdoor clothing store founded in 1897. Cross the street and stop at **Mox Boarding House** *(see p100)* for browsing through a range of classic and new board games. Visitors can play games and dine here as well. After a long morning in the shops, turn back and stop at **The Other Coast Café** *(see p101)* for its superb selection of East-Coast-style sandwiches.

See map on pp96–7 ←

Places to Shop

Furnishings on sale, Camelion Design

1 Camelion Design
MAP C1 ■ 5330 Ballard Ave NW ■ (206) 783-7125 ■ www.cameliondesign.com

An eclectic array of home furnishings, from sofas to lamps and candles, awaits at this contemporary home decor store.

2 Scandinavian Specialties
MAP C1 ■ 6719 15th Ave NW ■ www.scanspecialties.com

The place for all things Scandinavian, with a focus on Norwegian goods. Groceries, sweets, books, household items, and souvenirs are found here.

3 Fair Trade Winds
MAP B1 ■ 5329 Ballard Ave NW ■ (206) 743-8500 ■ www.fairtradewinds.net

This store sells fair-trade crafts from all around the world. It is a great place to find unusual Christmas ornaments.

4 Horseshoe
MAP B1 ■ 5344 Ballard Ave NW ■ www.shophorseshoe.com

Award-winning women's boutique with a well-chosen collection featuring both local and international designers. The friendly staff add to the charm.

5 Mox Boarding House
MAP C2 ■ 5105 Leary Ave NW ■ (206) 523-2273 ■ www.moxboardinghouse.com

Play board games in the café, or choose from the large selection for sale, both classic and unusual.

6 Secret Garden Books
MAP B1 ■ 2214 NW Market St ■ (206) 789-5006 ■ www.secretgardenbooks.com

This small neighborhood bookstore, which opened in 1977, has a great selection of new and used books. It also hosts events and readings.

7 Prism
MAP B1 ■ 5208 Ballard Ave NW ■ (206) 402-4706 ■ www.prismseattle.com

People come here for a selection of ultrahip clothing, accessories, cool bags and backpacks, and design pieces.

8 Dandelion Botanical Company
MAP B2 ■ 5424 Ballard Ave NW ■ (206) 545-8892 ■ www.dandelionbotanical.com

Opened in 1996, this urban herbal apothecary stocks organic herbs, medicinal oils and tinctures, teas, and bath and body supplies.

9 Lucca Great Finds
MAP B2 ■ 5332 Ballard Ave NW ■ (206) 782-7337 ■ www.luccagreatfinds.com

A rummage in this unique store turns up colorful candles, beautifully restored chandeliers, large old birdcages, antique cards, and maps.

10 re-soul
MAP C1 ■ 5319 Ballard Ave NW ■ (206) 789-7312 ■ www.resoul.com

This super stylish shoe store is known for its upscale European and American shoes. Also for sale are nifty bags, fashion accessories, and modern and retro home furnishings.

Places to Eat

PRICE CATEGORIES
Price categories include a three-course meal for one, two glasses of wine, and all unavoidable extra charges including tax.

$ under $40 $$ $40–80 $$$ over $80

1 Lockspot Café
MAP B1 ■ 3005 NW 54th
■ (206) 789-4865 ■ $

This café combines American staples at the busy takeout window, with a bar and a restaurant inside.

2 Hot Cakes
MAP B1
■ 5427 Ballard Ave
NW ■ (206) 453-3792 ■ $

Enjoy a delicious, gooey cake, with or without ice cream, or try one of the boozy milkshakes and ice cream floats at this popular spot.

Organic dessert, Hot Cakes

3 La Carta de Oaxaca
MAP B1 ■ 5431 Ballard Ave NW
■ (206) 782-8722 ■ Closed Sun ■ $

Make a beeline for this stylish Mexican eatery, and select from several entrees. The decor is unusual – wall art consists of backlit photos of the region from where all the flavors originate.

4 Hattie's Hat
MAP B1 ■ 5231 Ballard
Ave NW ■ (206) 784-0175 ■ $

A great place for huge breakfasts and classic American diner standards with a twist. The Guinness stout meatloaf, homemade creamed corn, sweet potato fries, and braised southern greens are worth a taste.

5 Salmon Bay Café
MAP B2 ■ 5109 Shilshole
Ave NW ■ (206) 782-5539
■ Closed D Sun–Wed ■ $

This bastion of inexpensive eats attracts groups of college students. The omelets are particularly popular.

6 The Other Coast Café
MAP B1 ■ 5315 Ballard Ave NW
■ (206) 789-0936 ■ Closed D ■ $

Stick to basics such as the Reuben or the 14-inch meat or vegetarian subs at this New York-style deli.

7 India Bistro
MAP B1 ■ 2301 NW Market St
■ (206) 783-5080 ■ $

Recommended dishes here include spinach or mustard greens with paneer, spicy daal, and succulent lamb or chicken tandoori.

8 The Walrus and the Carpenter
MAP C2 ■ 4743 Ballard Ave NW ■ (206) 395-9227 ■ $$

A tiny place (see p57) that serves mounds of oysters and fresh seafood.

9 Ray's Boathouse & Café
MAP A1 ■ 6049 Seaview Ave NW ■ (206) 789-3770 ■ $$ (café); $$$ (boathouse)

Classic seafood dishes and waterfront views make this a favorite (see p56).

Diners eating at Stoneburner

10 Stoneburner
MAP B2 ■ 5214 Ballard Ave NW ■ (206) 695-2051 ■ www.stoneburnerseattle.com ■ $$$

A top restaurant for fresh seafood, wood-fired pizza, and a cocktail menu with non-alcoholic options.

See map on pp96–7

TOP 10 West Seattle

A stretch of Elliott Bay separates central Seattle from the peninsula of West Seattle, the city's oldest and largest district. Connected by a high freeway bridge and a lower span, West Seattle's proximity to both downtown and the Industrial District has always made it a popular residential area. It has attracted a population of younger, entrepreneurial residents drawn by lower housing costs and some of the best parklands in the city. Alki Beach brings hordes of people when the long, damp winter months give way to sunnier spring days.

Alki Point Lighthouse

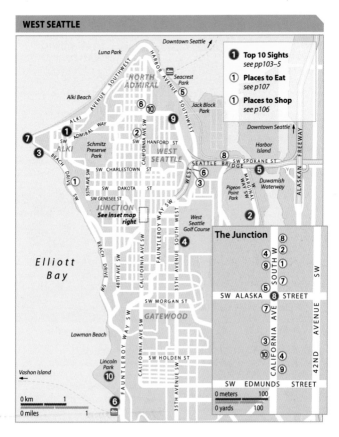

WEST SEATTLE

1	Top 10 Sights see pp103–5
1	Places to Eat see p107
1	Places to Shop see p106

1 Log House Museum
MAP A5 ■ 3003 61st Ave SW ■ (206) 350-0999 ■ Open noon–4pm Fri–Sun ■ Suggested donation: $3 (adult), $1 (child); tours $2 ■ www.loghousemuseum.org

The museum, near Alki Beach, takes local history seriously. It marks the location where Captain Folger steered his schooner *Exact* in 1851, bringing to the region the families of Seattle's earliest pioneers, including the Arthur A. Denny party *(see p36)*. The museum explores the history of the Duwamish Peninsula with an orientation center, exhibits that preserve the community's legacy, speaker programs, and some special events.

2 Duwamish Longhouse and Cultural Center
MAP B6 ■ 4705 W Marginal Way SW ■ (206) 431-1582 ■ Open 10am–5pm Tue–Sat ■ www.duwamishtribe.org

This longhouse is a replica of the one which was used by the ancient Duwamish tribe for thousands of years before Seattle became a city. Cultural and educational events are held here and provide a fascinating insight into how the culture of this Indigenous Tribe has evolved over time.

3 Constellation Park
MAP A5 ■ 3521 Beach Dr SW ■ (206) 684-4075

Seattle beachcombers check for the year's lowest tides and head to one of the best shoreline secrets, Constellation Park. It is not the best recreational shore, because it lacks a wide sandy stretch, but it gets its name from the large number of fascinating sea stars (starfish) that cling onto the rocky intertidal zone. If the conditions are right, it is common to find scores of colorful sea stars, along with the usual anemones, gargantuan sea snails, as well as geoducks, Puget Sound's giant clams.

Totem pole, Log House Museum

4 Camp Long
MAP B6 ■ 5200 35th SW ■ (206) 684-7434

In spite of being located in an entirely urban locale, Camp Long manages to come close to imparting the exciting wild and natural experiences that are usually found only during hikes in the local mountain ranges. At one point in time, this 1941-era camp served only scouting organizations. However, in 1984, the large compound was made open to the general public. Inside the camp's grounds, visitors can hike through trails, learn about the environment from professional naturalists, or even rent charming cabins for inner-city camping. A popular attraction here is the 20-ft- (6-m-) high Schurman climbing rock, carefully designed to incorporate every climbing maneuver. Bats, northern flying squirrels, opossums, raccoons, and chipmunks have been sighted within the camp's area. Weekly interpretive walks, rock-climbing classes, and a golf course are also available.

A cabin in Camp Long

5 West Seattle Bridge
MAP B5

From downtown, the fastest way to anywhere in West Seattle is via this highway crossing, built in 1984. The bridge takes traffic from the inter-state I-5 and other feeder streets over the artificial Harbor Island and the mouth of the Duwamish River, and through to all the major streets in West Seattle. It is visible from many vantage points in town.

The scenic Fauntleroy Ferry Terminal

DREDGING THE DUWAMISH

Before European settlers landed in what would become Seattle, the Duwamish River zigzagged throughout the valley between the hillsides of West Seattle and Beacon Hill to the east. The area was in many ways more wetland than river until the Army Corps of Engineers dredged it in the late 19th century, deepening the bed and making the Duwamish permanently navigable by large commercial vessels. The dredge created Harbor Island, which lies in between two small channels where the Duwamish pours into Elliott Bay.

6 Fauntleroy Ferry Terminal
MAP P3

The Fauntleroy Ferry is the only ferry from Seattle that travels to the pastoral Vashon Island, and its terminal is located at the end of Fauntleroy Way. Unlike the down-town terminal, this one is located in a residential neighborhood, adjacent to scenic Lincoln Park (see p44). Allow some time to walk along the water's edge to watch ferries come and go. For a memo-rable visit to Vashon, bring along a bike, and visit the lovely pick-yourself berry patches in summer.

7 Alki Point
MAP A5

Seattle pioneer Arthur A. Denny (see p36) and his party aboard the ship *Exact* were the first Europeans to settle in the region. They chose the beachhead of West Seattle to come ashore in 1851, and were met on arrival by the Duwamish Tribe Chief Sealth (see p37). Today, Alki Point boasts rows of upscale waterfront condos for the well-to-do, and a great beach for shell hunting or scuba diving.

Waterfront path, Alki Beach

8 The Junction
MAP A6

The name refers to the intersection where California Avenue and Alaska Street meet, and it is here that the bulk of West Seattle's restaurants and shops are located. The small-town feel is palpable as you stroll along California Avenue past mom 'n' pop shops, and notice old-timers out for walks or sipping coffee at sidewalk tables. Murals painted on the sides of businesses mirror the warmth and pride of a tight-knit community in its prime, and reflect on its 150-year-old history.

Blossoming flora at Belvedere Park

9 Belvedere Park Viewpoint
MAP B5 ■ 3600 SW Admiral Way

For a bird's-eye view of the city of Seattle and the countryside beyond, simply drive or take a bus up Admiral Way to tiny Belvedere Park. Take in 180-degree picture-postcard views of the Cascade Range behind the high-rises of downtown, industrial Harbor Island, and the Port of Seattle's con-tainer yards, as well as Puget Sound and Elliott Bay. On clear days, the dis-tant and permanently snowcapped Mount Baker on the northeastern horizon looms above all else.

10 Lincoln Park
MAP P3 ■ 8011 Fauntleroy Way SW

Set close to Puget Sound, this large park with athletic fields and picnic areas offers views of the Sound and the Ferry. A paved walking trail, bordered with tall evergreens, runs along the beach. Its heated saltwater pool is open to the public in summer.

A MORNING AT ALKI BEACH

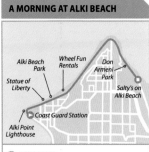

▶ MORNING

Experience the scenic Alki Avenue via a leisurely walk and easy bike ride along a waterfront trail (about 3.5 miles – 5.5 km – each way). Begin at the **Coast Guard Station** *(3201 Alki Ave)* which offers tours of the **Alki Point Lighthouse** on Sundays from June to August (1–4pm). Walking northeast, stop at 63rd Ave SW to see the monument erected to celebrate the arrival of Seattle's early settlers. At 61st Ave SW, just before **Alki Beach Park** begins, look for the miniature **Statue of Liberty** on the right, built in 1952 on the strip of land dubbed "New York Alki" by the early settlers.

The sandy stretch of Alki Beach begins around 60th Ave. Stroll until 53rd Ave while taking in the views of Puget Sound, its ships and sailboats to the north, and the Olympic Mountains to the west. Rent a beach bike nearby at **Wheel Fun Rentals** *(see p111)* and continue along the trail. Public restrooms are available at the intersection of 57th Ave SW. As the road curves and becomes Harbor Ave, have a look through the telescopes set up above the seawall for more great views. Near the 1100 block of Harbor Ave look out for **Don Armeni Park**, where wedding parties and professional photographers often congregate to snap pictures of the city skyline. Stop at **Salty's on Alki Beach** *(see p107)* for a seriously scrumptious brunch that includes an all-you-can-eat Dungeness crab and other seafood indulgences.

See map on p102 ←

Places to Shop

Trendy accessories, homeware, and stationery for sale at Click! Design That Fits

1 **Click! Design that Fits**
MAP B5 ▪ 4540 California Ave SW ▪ (206) 328-9252 ▪ www.clickdesignthatfits.com

Meticulously designed paper crafts, books, kitchen goods, interior design items, and artwork are sold here.

2 **Carmilia's**
MAP A6 ▪ 4528 California Ave SW ▪ (206) 935-1329 ▪ www.shopcarmilias.com

A boutique clothing store selling an assortment of locally crafted jewelry, body care products and accessories, along with luxurious beach wear.

3 **Northwest Art & Frame**
MAP A6 ▪ 4733 California Ave SW ▪ (206) 937-5507

This welcoming store offers an enormous selection of custom and ready-made frames, art supplies, cards, stationery, and gift items.

4 **Thunder Road Guitars**
MAP B5 ▪ 4736 California Ave SW ▪ (206) 678-5248 ▪ www.thunderroadguitars.com

Beautifully restored electric and acoustic guitars are available here. Snap up the cables, and all the extras.

5 **Easy Street Records**
MAP A6 ▪ 4559 California Ave SW ▪ (206) 938-3279 ▪ www.easystreetonline.com

Shop here for the latest indie rock albums, then stop for lunch and an espresso in the café.

6 **Avalon Glassworks**
MAP B5 ▪ 2914 SW Avalon Way ▪ (206) 937-6369

Talented artists create blown-glass vases, sculptures, and ornaments, in myriad shapes, colors, and sizes at this exciting workshop.

7 **Pharmaca Integrative Pharmacy**
MAP A6 ▪ 4707 California Ave SW ▪ (206) 932-4225 ▪ www.pharmaca.com

The professional and personalized service here focuses on wellness.

8 **West Seattle Computers**
MAP A6 ▪ 2735 California Ave SW ▪ (206) 937-6800

The technical staff at this computer store are as friendly as they are tech savvy. Buy software or hardware, or have any digital problems solved.

9 **Curious Kidstuff**
MAP A6 ▪ 4740 California Ave SW ▪ (206) 937-8788 ▪ www.curiouskidstuff.com

Find all manner of treasures for children at this fun and welcoming toy store. There is a large selection of eco-friendly and wooden toys.

10 **Metropolitan Market**
MAP B5 ▪ 2320 42nd Ave SW ▪ (206) 937-0551 ▪ $

This neighborhood supermarket and gourmet purveyor of prepared food sells a good selection of pasta dishes, paninis and customized salads. The store also sells quality kitchenware.

Places to Eat

PRICE CATEGORIES
Price categories include a three-course meal for one, two glasses of wine, and all unavoidable extra charges including tax.

$ under $40 $$ $40–80 $$$ over $80

1 La Rustica
MAP A5 ▪ 4100 Beach Drive SW ▪ (206) 932-3020 ▪ $$

Dine on exquisite Italian classics, such as spaghetti with garlic prawns, or pizza with mushrooms and prosciutto ham.

2 Arthur's
MAP B5 ▪ 2311 California Ave SW ▪ (206) 829-8235 ▪ $$

Indulge in a hearty brunch featuring avocado toast and crab eggs Benedict at this Australian-inspired spot. Lunch and dinner menus offer comfort food.

3 Luna Park Café
MAP B5 ▪ 2918 SW Avalon Way ▪ (206) 935-7250 ▪ $

The kitschy artifacts and retro-style decor at Luna Park Café recreate a charming setting from the 1950s. Popular basics feature on the menu, including flavorsome BLT and club sandwiches, hand-dipped malted milkshakes, and classic cobb salad.

4 Azuma Sushi
MAP A6 ▪ 4533 California Ave SW ▪ (206) 937-1148 ▪ Closed Sun ▪ $

Insiders return here often for their fix of professionally prepared sushi and sashimi, sake, and teriyaki at very reasonable prices.

5 Salty's on Alki Beach
MAP B5 ▪ 1936 Harbor Ave SW ▪ (206) 937-1600 ▪ $$

The specials board at Salty's lists the freshest seasonal fish and seafood available, and picture windows offer diners the most breathtaking views across Elliott Bay.

6 Mission Cantina
MAP A5 ▪ 2325 California Ave SW ▪ (206) 937-8220 ▪ $

Head to Mission for Latin American food and great margaritas.

7 Jak's Grill
MAP A6 ▪ 4548 California Ave SW ▪ (206) 937-7809 ▪ $$

This steakhouse prepares superb beef, chicken, and seafood dishes. The price includes many side orders.

8 Chelan Café
MAP B5 ▪ 3527 Chelan Ave SW ▪ (206) 932-7383 ▪ Closed D ▪ $

Burger, Chelan Café

Dine on typical, good-value American truck-stop fare here, including burgers, fries, meatloaf, and eggs.

9 West 5
MAP A6 ▪ 4539 California Ave SW ▪ (206) 935-1966 ▪ $

Munch on comfort food such as BLTs and burgers at this hip eatery.

Desserts at Bakery Nouveau

10 Bakery Nouveau
MAP A6 ▪ 4737 California Ave SW ▪ (206) 923-0534 ▪ Closed D ▪ $

This award-winning bakery always has lines for its inviting assortment of fresh, buttery, flaky treats. The friendly staff also serve gourmet coffee drinks and delicious pizzas.

See map on p102

Streetsmart

Neon food stall signs along
Seattle's Pike Place Market

Getting Around

Arriving by Air

Sea-Tac International Airport (SEA) lies about 10 miles (16 km) south of Seattle and is served by dozens of carriers, including British Airways, Delta, and Lufthansa, along with budget airlines, such as Southwest Air. There are non-stop flights from London, Frankfurt, Paris, Amsterdam, and a few other European hubs, and non-stop flights to Hong Kong, Shanghai, Beijing, Seoul, and Tokyo. The easiest way to get into Seattle is via light rail – follow the signs from baggage claim. Trains run approximately every 6–15 minutes and take about 40 minutes to reach downtown. Buses also run to the city center. Purchase tickets in advance using the Transit GO Ticket app.

Arriving by Seaplane

Kenmore Air has a fleet of seaplanes that offer tours of Puget Sound, the Cascades to the east, and the Olympic Mountains to the west. Kenmore also serves several destinations in British Columbia, Canada. Flights land on the water in Lake Union, just north of downtown.

Buses

Bolt Bus runs express services from Seattle to Portland or Vancouver, Canada. **Greyhound** also has an extensive network of buses; they stop more frequently so travel times can be longer.

Trains

Seattle's King Street Station is the depot for **Amtrak** passenger trains from Vancouver, British Columbia, and all points south and east. The Coast Starlight travels between Los Angeles and Seattle, and the Amtrak Cascades itineraries serve stops between Eugene, Oregon, and Vancouver. Although the Cascades line is reliable, the Coast Starlight regularly experiences delays; it is not the best choice for those needing to make a connection in another destination. Be aware that Amtrak runs buses rather than trains on some of its routes.

Commuter Rail

Seattle's commuter rail service, **Sound Transit**, links King Street Station with Everett, Edmonds, Kent, Sumner, Auburn, Tukwila, Puyallup, and Tacoma. Service is limited, though; check online for the relevant time schedule.

Ferries

For a fantastic way to experience Seattle and its environs, consider taking a ferry. Major routes operated by **Washington State Ferries** include: Seattle-Bremerton and Seattle-Winslow (on Bainbridge Island) from Pier 52, and West Seattle-Vashon Island and West Seattle-Southworth from the Fauntleroy terminal. There is a shuttle that takes ferry passengers from the ferry dock in West Seattle to the Alki Beach business district and the Alaska Junction business district, which is free with a ferry ticket. From Anacortes, some distance north of Seattle, there is a ferry service to the San Juan Islands and Sydney (on Vancouver Island, north of Victoria).

Public Transit

King County Metro Transit offers the most affordable transportation option. Pay on entry for buses heading downtown, and on leaving for buses heading away from downtown. If connecting with another bus, ask for a free transfer from the driver. Most buses are equipped with wheelchair lifts. King County Metro Transit includes the light rail, with its service to Sea-Tac, and the South Lake Union Trolley.

Be sure to purchase a regional transit ORCA card from the Westlake Tunnel transit station or the metro customer service office downtown, open 8:30am to 4:30pm, Monday to Friday. Tickets and cards for buses are available from machines at most light rail stations.

Car and Taxi

There are plenty of rental car counters at the airport, but most rental lots are located offsite and are reachable by shuttle from the arrivals level. There are several rental car lots downtown for those who do not need a car for their entire trip – also avoiding the airport surcharge. If reserving a car in advance, make sure to select a downtown pickup location.

Popular car rental firms include **Enterprise Rent-A-Car**, **Avis**, and **National Car Rental**. Insurance is required, which can be purchased from the rental company for those who do not already have cover. A car can be handy, but in the heart of downtown Seattle it may be more trouble than it is worth. Traffic is usually heavy and parking expensive – a **Seattle Yellow Cab** is often a better option. App-based car-sharing services, such as **Uber** and **Lyft**, are common in the city. It costs about $45 for a taxi from the airport to the downtown hotel district.

Cycling

Seattle's hilly landscape means biking is not necessarily the best option, but there are a few easy trails along Alki Beach in West Seattle (see p104), and more adventurous cyclists can try out the Burke-Gilman Trail (see p93) to Redmond, 16 miles (25 km) east of the city; it can also be walked. A downloadable **Seattle Bike Map**, showcasing cycling routes across the city, can be found on the city council website.

Cyclists are much safer on paths reserved for non-motorized vehicles. There is a city-wide law that requires riders to wear helmets. A good rental company is **Wheel Fun Rentals**. Some hotels have free loaner bicycles, so ask at the front desk.

Walking

As with cycling, Seattle's hills and stair climbs can be daunting, but walking is nonetheless a great way to explore the city. Walking tours led by **Seattle Architecture Foundation** explore the University of Washington campus, Pike Place Market, and the architecture and history of Pioneer Square; there are also a wide range of food tours, including through the Chinatown-International District. The city council offers a downloadable **Seattle Walking Map** on its website, which outlines different routes; handily, the city's steeper streets have been shaded in yellow. **TrailLink** also offers dozens of maps for walking and hiking in and around the city.

DIRECTORY

ARRIVING BY AIR

Sea-Tac International Airport (SEA)
17801 International Blvd
ⓦ portseattle.org/Sea-Tac

ARRIVING BY SEAPLANE

Kenmore Air
ⓦ kenmoreair.com

BUSES

Bolt Bus
ⓦ boltbus.com

Greyhound
ⓦ greyhound.com

TRAINS

Amtrak
MAP K6 ▪ 303 S
Jackson St
ⓦ amtrak.com

COMMUTER RAIL

Sound Transit
ⓦ soundtransit.org

FERRIES

Washington State Ferries
ⓦ wsdot.wa.gov/ferries

PUBLIC TRANSIT

King County Metro Transit
ⓦ kingcounty.gov/depts/transportation/metro.aspx

CAR AND TAXI

Avis
ⓦ avis.com

Enterprise Rent-A-Car
ⓦ enterprise.com

Lyft
ⓦ lyft.com

National Car Rental
MAP K4 ▪ 1601 3rd Ave
ⓦ nationalcar.com

Seattle Yellow Cab
ⓦ seattleyellowcab.com

Uber
ⓦ uber.com

CYCLING

Seattle Bike Map
ⓦ seattle.gov/transportation

Wheel Fun Rentals
MAP A5 ▪ 2530
Alki Ave
ⓦ wheelfunrentals.com

WALKING

Seattle Architecture Foundation
ⓦ seattlearchitecture.org

Seattle Walking Map
ⓦ seattle.gov/transportation

TrailLink
ⓦ traillink.com/city/seattle-wa-trails

Practical Information

Passports and Visas

For entry requirements, including visas, consult your nearest US embassy or check with the **US Department of State**. Canadian citizens require a valid passport to enter the US. Visitors from Australia, New Zealand, Japan, the UK, and the EU do not need a visa, but must apply well in advance (and pay a fee) for the **ESTA** (Electronic System for Travel Authorization) and have a valid passport to enter. Other nationalities must have a valid passport and tourist visa to enter. A return airline ticket is required to enter the US.

Government Advice

Now more than ever, it is important to consult both your and the US government's advice before travelling. The **UK Foreign and Commonwealth Office**, US Department of State, and **Australian Department of Foreign Affairs and Trade** offer the latest information on security, health, and local regulations.

Customs Information

You can find information on the laws relating to goods and currency taken in or out of the US on the **Customs and Border Protection Agency** website.

Insurance

We recommend that you take out a comprehensive insurance policy covering theft, loss of belongings, medical care, cancellations and delays, and read the small print carefully.

Health

The US has a world-class healthcare system. However, there is no universal healthcare available and costs for medical and dental care can be high. Comprehensive medical insurance is therefore highly recommended for international travelers to the US.

For information regarding COVID-19 vaccination requirements, consult government advice. No other inoculations are required for visiting the US.

All city hospitals have walk-in emergency rooms. Recommended hospitals include the **Virginia Mason Hospital** and **Harborview Medical Center**. For less critical issues, minor injuries, illness, or sexual health issues, look for urgent care clinics at Bartell's or Walgreen's convenience stores.

Many big supermarkets have pharmacies on site, as do Rite Aid, and the Walgreen's and Bartell's convenience stores. The pharmacist can usually advise on simple health problems. You should not have trouble finding the medication you need, but bring a doctor's letter and a copy of any prescription to avoid problems. Make a note of the generic name, as well as the brand name, of the required medication. Drugs in the US can be expensive, so it is wise to prepare in advance by bringing extra medication from home.

Smoking, Alcohol, and Drugs

The legal age for drinking alcohol in the US is 21; you will need photo ID as proof of age in order to buy alcohol and enter bars.

Purchase of cigarettes, tobacco, and vapor products is legal for adults 21 and older; proof of age will be required. It is illegal to smoke in all public spaces and workspaces.

In Washington, marijuana use is legal for adults over 21 years. It must be consumed in private and can only be purchased at state-licensed retail stores using photo ID.

There are strict fines for driving under the influence of marijuana or alcohol.

ID

There is no requirement for visitors to carry ID in Seattle, but due to occasional checks you may be asked to show a photocopy of your passport or other picture ID.

Personal Security

Although much of Seattle is safe for visitors, there are areas, as in any city, that may not be especially tourist friendly. Use your common sense and be alert to your surroundings, and you should enjoy a trouble-free trip.

If you have anything stolen, report the crime within 24 hours to the nearest police station and take ID with you. Get a copy of the crime report in order to claim on your insurance. Contact your embassy if you have your passport stolen, or in the event of a serious crime or accident.

As a rule, Seattleites are very accepting of all people, regardless of their race, gender, or sexuality. Washington state legalised same-sex marriage in 2012, gave its citizens the right to legally change their gender in 2017, and in 2019 offered "X" as a gender marker on ID and driver's licenses.

The Seattle Police Department's Safe Place initiative is a network of businesses and groups committed to protecting victims of bias or hate crimes and providing them with a safe place if they feel unsafe. Participating businesses have a police badge-shaped, rainbow-striped Safe Place sticker on their storefronts.

The **emergency services** (fire, police, and ambulance) can be contacted by dialling 911.

Travelers with Specific Requirements

Seattle's King County Metro Transit *(see p111)* and many other attractions offer discounted fares for travelers with specific requirements. The Regional Reduced Fare Permit costs $3 and entitles you to reduced fares on Community Transit, Metro Transit, Washington State Ferries, and Sound Transit. Obtaining this pass will require an **American Disabilities Act (ADA) Paratransit Card**.

Drivers with specific requirements may park in designated spaces if they have the proper vehicle identification from the **Department of Licensing**. National parks also issue vehicle passes that entitle all a vehicle's passengers to enter the park for free.

Seattle's metro system pioneered the use of Lift-U lifts on buses for those with limited mobility. Look out for a wheelchair symbol posted on placards at

bus stops. Every downtown corner provides ramped curbs, while most government buildings, supermarkets, tourist attractions, performance venues, and hotels have hands-free doorways and access ramps.

Many of Seattle's major attractions offer services for travelers with specific requirements. Both the Seattle Space Needle and Pike Place Market have lifts for those with limited mobility, while the Seattle Art Museum has magnifiers, ASL public tours, and assistive listening devices; in addition, those who are visually impaired can experience the exhibits through the Art Beyond Sight Tour.

Visit Seattle *(see p115)* has further information on the city's accessible sights. **Wheelchair Travel** offers details on transport, accommodations, and sights, and **Sight Connection Community Services for the Blind and Partially Sighted** is a great resource for sight-impaired individuals.

DIRECTORY

PASSPORTS AND VISAS

ESTA
🅦 esta.cbp.dhs.gov

US Department of State
🅦 travel.state.gov

GOVERNMENT ADVICE

Australian Department of Foreign Affairs and Trade
🅦 smartraveller.gov.au

UK Foreign and Commonwealth Office
🅦 gov.uk/foreign-travel-advice

CUSTOMS INFORMATION

Customs and Border Protection Agency
🅦 cbp.gov/travel

HEALTH

Harborview Medical Center
MAP L5 ▪ 325 9th Ave
📞 (206) 744-3000

Virginia Mason Hospital
MAP L4 ▪ 925 Seneca St
📞 (206) 624-1144

PERSONAL SECURITY

Emergency Services
📞 911

TRAVELERS WITH SPECIFIC REQUIREMENTS

American Disabilities Act (ADA) Paratransit Card
🅦 metro.kingcounty.gov

Department of Licensing
🅦 dol.wa.gov

Sight Connection Community Services for the Blind and Partially Sighted
🅦 sightconnection.org

Wheelchair Travel
🅦 wheelchairtravel.org/seattle/

Time Zone

Seattle keeps Pacific Standard Time (PST), eight hours behind GMT and three hours behind Eastern Standard Time (EST). Daylight saving time is observed between March and November.

Money

The US currency is the dollar. Most establishments accept major credit, debit, and prepaid currency cards. Contactless payments are becoming increasingly common, but cash is usually required by smaller shops and businesses. ATMs can be found at most banks and around the city. Look out for currency exchange offices in the main terminal and South Satellite at the Sea-Tac Airport, as well as at major banks downtown. Avoid bad exchange rates by withdrawing cash from ATMs around town, where daily rates are more advantageous. There may be a small fee to use the ATM for those who are not customers of the bank (their own bank may charge, too). Check with the bank for charges before traveling.

Tipping is customary in the US. In restaurants it is normal to tip 20 per cent of the total bill. Allow for a tip of 15–20 per cent for taxi drivers and bar staff. Hotel porters and housekeeping expect $2–$3 per bag or day.

Electrical Appliances

American current puts out 110 volts compared to Europe's 220. Almost all new appliances run dual voltage, but the outlets are a different shape so an adapter will be needed. Check device manuals to be sure. Most hotels, vacation rentals, and B&Bs supply hair dryers.

Cell Phones and Wi-Fi

Cell phone service in Seattle is generally good. In order to use your phone abroad you may need to activate the "roaming" facility. Other options include buying a prepaid cell phone in the US or a SIM chip for a US carrier.

Seattle's area code is 206, but the vastness of surrounding suburbs has necessitated several prefixes. The Eastside (see pp42–3) is mostly covered by 425, while 253 covers south of the city, and 360 handles outlying areas. To call outside the 206 area code, dial 1, the area code, and the seven-digit number. Toll-free phone numbers begin with 800, 877, or 888. Dial 411 for directory assistance, 011 for an international call.

Home to tech giants such as Microsoft and Amazon, Seattle offers exceptional internet facilities. Wi-Fi is available at Sea-Tac, libraries, and coffee shops. A number of restaurants and hotels offer Wi-Fi too, although the latter may charge a small fee.

Postal Services

The **Main Post Office** is located at Third and Union in downtown. Almost all post offices have automated mailing stations where customers can weigh their items and buy postage without standing in line. Some drug stores, convenience stores, and supermarkets will also sell stamps, but they may not have proper international postage. Postcards cost $1.15 to send abroad.

Opening Hours

Department stores and supermarkets are open daily, and a few larger ones stay open till 10pm on some nights. Banks are usually open 8am to 5pm Monday to Friday, but ATMs are accessible at all times. Post offices are open 9am to 5pm Monday to Friday. Museums are open 10am to 5pm, but often stay open until 9pm one night a week. Bars will serve liquor until 2am.

COVID-19 Increased rates of infection may result in temporary opening hours and/or closures. Always check ahead before visiting museums, attractions and hospitality venues.

Weather

July is historically the driest month of the year, and late spring, summer, and early fall are the most mild and appealing times to visit. Most festivals and street fairs occur during the summer. Be prepared for rain all year round. Winter is the least popular season to visit, making it ideal for travelers seeking affordable hotel rates and fewer crowds. The colder months also attract many skiers and other snow sports enthusiasts.

Visitor Information

Visit Seattle provides excellent information for a visit to Seattle, while **Washington State Tourism** is helpful for information on the rest of the state.

The Stranger and the *Seattle Weekly* both have great information online about events and activities. These free local papers can be found in cafés and corner news-boxes. The **Seattle Eater** is an up-to-date online source for the restaurant and bar scene.

The **Seattle CityPass** provides discounted entry to some of Seattle's biggest attractions, including the Space Needle and Museum of Pop Culture.

Language

English is the official language in Seattle. Other languages include Chinese and Spanish, both spoken by around 4 per cent of the population.

Taxes and Refunds

The current sales tax in Seattle is 10.5 per cent;

it is charged on all retail purchases. As this tax is not levied at a national level, tourists cannot claim sales tax refunds.

Trips and Tours

There are many options for touring Seattle and the region. Walking tours help visitors explore Pike Place Market and the Chinatown-International District *(see p111)*, **Seattle by Segway** runs tours along the beach at Alki, **Argosy Cruises** takes visitors through the Ballard Locks, and **Alki Kayak Tours** ventures out to see the orcas that live in Puget Sound. Tour operators will also take tourists to harder-to-reach places, such as Mount Rainier and the Boeing Aircraft Factory.

Accommodation

Major hotel chains, plus a few boutique offerings, are located primarily downtown and around the Seattle Center. Capitol Hill has the highest concentration of B&Bs and smaller inns, with many set in beautifully renovated classic homes. East

Capitol Hill is quieter than downtown, while still being convenient to transit, and often, parking is included.

Vacation rentals are available all over the city, from single rooms in private homes to entire apartments. The cheapest stays will usually be at hostels. There are five in Seattle; offerings run from private rooms to shared bunks with a communal bathroom down the hall.

Seattle's occupancy rates are usually high, making last-minute bargains rare. It is therefore best to reserve in advance, especially during summer and fall. Rooms under $200 per night are considered a good deal in Seattle – while standard and boutique hotels can start as high as $600 per night. Basic hostel bunks are about $30 per night.

In Seattle, there is a tax of 15.7 per cent on the total cost of a hotel stay; this is charged at the end of your stay, once all extras (such as room service) have been taken into account. In addition, a further $2 is charged per night per room.

DIRECTORY

POSTAL SERVICES

Main Post Office
MAP K4 ■ 301 Union St
■ (206) 748-5417

VISITOR INFORMATION

Seattle Eater
🌐 seattle.eater.com

Seattle Weekly
🌐 seattleweekly.com

Seattle CityPass
🌐 citypass.com/seattle

The Stranger
🌐 thestranger.com

Visit Seattle
MAP K4 ■ 701 Pike St
🌐 visitseattle.org

Washington State Tourism
🌐 experiencewa.com

TRIPS AND TOURS

Alki Kayak Tours
MAP B5 ■ 1660 Harbor Ave SW
🌐 kayakalki.com

Argosy Cruises
MAP J5 ■ 1101 Alaskan Way, Pier 55
🌐 argosycruises.com

Seattle by Segway
🌐 seattlebysegway.com

Places to Stay

PRICE CATEGORIES

For a standard, double room per night (with breakfast if included), taxes, and extra charges.

$ under $250	$$ $250–350	$$$ over $350

Downtown Hotels

Belltown Inn

MAP J3 ▪ 2301 3rd Ave ▪ (206) 529-3700 ▪ www.belltown-inn.com ▪ $

Located in the heart of hip Belltown, this complex features fully furnished studios with kitchenettes. Bikes are available free of charge. It is a short walk from Pike Place Market and is on the free Metro bus line.

Courtyard Seattle Downtown/Lake Union

MAP J1 ▪ 925 Westlake Ave N ▪ (206) 213-0100 ▪ www.marriott.com ▪ $

One of Marriott's less expensive offerings, this hotel has great lake views. Rooms have free internet, and there is also a fitness center on site. The hotel is walking distance from the streetcar to downtown.

Hotel Theodore

MAP K4 ▪ 1531 7th Ave ▪ (206) 621-1200 ▪ www.hoteltheodore.com ▪ $

This hotel is located near downtown's best shopping spots. Evenings bring live jazz piano to the lobby, where visitors gather to relax and mingle.

Best Western Plus Pioneer Square

MAP K5 ▪ 77 Yesler Way ▪ (206) 340-1234 ▪ www.pioneersquare.com ▪ $$

History buffs and sports fans flock to this quaint 19th-century hotel featuring period decor and deluxe bathrooms. The waterfront, ferry terminal, stadiums, and Pioneer Square are all nearby.

Grand Hyatt Seattle

MAP K3 ▪ 721 Pine St ▪ (206) 774-1234 ▪ www.grandseattle.hyatt.com ▪ $$

The deluxe rooms include free use of the sprawling health club, which has an exercise room, a sauna, a Jacuzzi, a steam room, and cardio machines with flat-screen televisions.

Hilton Seattle

MAP K4 ▪ 1301 6th Ave ▪ (206) 624-0500 ▪ www.thehiltonseattle.com ▪ $$

Set near the Convention Center, the Hilton is very popular with business travelers. All rooms are above the 14th floor, with fantastic views, and there is free web TV. Check out the senior citizen and family discount plans. There is also a rental car company located on site.

Hotel Ändra

MAP J3 ▪ 2000 4th Ave ▪ (206) 448-8600 ▪ www.hotelandra.com ▪ $$

Top-notch service and a boutique experience are offered at this sophisticated hotel. Scandinavian design elements can be seen in all of the 119 rooms and luxury suites.

Hotel Max

MAP K3 ▪ 620 Stewart St ▪ (206) 728-6299 ▪ www.hotelmaxseattle.com ▪ $$

A stylish boutique hotel decorated with original artwork by local artists. Head to the lobby for locally roasted coffee in the morning or a selection of microbrews at happy hour. The on-site restaurant serves terrific grilled fare and seafood, as well as cocktails.

Kimpton Hotel Vintage Seattle

MAP K4 ▪ 1100 5th Ave ▪ 1-800-853-3914 ▪ www.hotelvintage-seattle.com ▪ $$

Comforts at this upscale hotel include plush terrycloth robes, lush fabrics, and cherry wood furniture. Guests can also enjoy a hosted wine hour by a wood-burning fireplace in the lobby. Try Tulio, the award-winning Italian restaurant for a sumptuous dinner.

Mayflower Park Hotel

MAP J4 ▪ 405 Olive Way ▪ 1-800-426-5100 ▪ www.mayflowerpark.com ▪ $$

The Mayflower was built in 1927. Rooms reflect common 1920s Queen Anne design touches in subtle and dark hues. The house restaurant is Andaluca, a small, top-rated establishment offering Mediterranean fare. The adjoining bar, Oliver's, serves exquisite martinis and cocktails.

Renaissance Seattle

MAP K5 ▪ 515 Madison St ▪ (206) 583-0300 ▪ www.marriott.com ▪ $$

A deluxe pet-friendly hotel with a 24-hour fitness center, modern ocean-view rooms, as well as a welcoming bar.

Seattle Marriott Waterfront

MAP H4 ▪ 2100 Alaskan Way ▪ (206) 443-5000 ▪ www.marriott.com ▪ $$

Seattle's first full-service hotel offers excellent views of Puget Sound and the snowy Olympic Mountains. There is a fitness center and a great restaurant serving craft beer and artisanal wines.

The Westin Seattle

MAP K3 ▪ 1900 5th Ave ▪ (206) 728-1000 ▪ www.marriott.com ▪ $$

Located in two towers, the Westin has an indoor pool, fitness suite, 24-hour room service, a restaurant and lobby bar, valet and laundry, as well as a business center.

W Seattle

MAP K4 ▪ 1112 4th Ave ▪ (206) 264-6000 ▪ www.wseattle.com ▪ $$

The sleek W attracts hip, well-heeled folk. It offers modern amenities, impeccable hospitality (that includes the W's signature "Whatever/Whenever" concierge service), and divinely comfortable beds.

Alexis Royal Sonesta Hotel

MAP K5 ▪ 1007 1st Ave ▪ 1-866-356-8894 ▪ www.sonesta.com ▪ $$$

Since 1901, the hotel has lived up to its reputation as an elegant haven. Evening wine tasting, 24-hour room service, a gym with a rock-climbing wall, a full-day spa, and the Bookstore Bar are highlights.

The Edgewater Hotel

MAP H4 ▪ 2411 Alaskan Way, Pier 67 ▪ 1-800-624-0670 ▪ www.edgewaterhotel.com ▪ $$$

All rooms combine luxury with Pacific Northwest charm. Features include handcrafted pine furniture, gas fireplaces, deluxe bathroom amenities, and an in-room coffee service.

Fairmont Olympic Hotel

MAP K4 ▪ 411 University St ▪ 1-888-363-5022 ▪ www.fairmont.com ▪ $$$

One of Pacific Northwest's most lauded properties, this landmark hotel has treated guests with the utmost elegance and personalized service since it opened in 1924.

Hotel 1000

MAP K4 ▪ 1000 1st Ave ▪ (206) 957-1000 ▪ www.hotel1000seattle.com ▪ $$$

An upscale hotel set in a great downtown location. Rooms feature fine Thai linens and state-of-the-art entertainment centers. The All Water Seafood & Oyster Bar here promises a memorable experience.

Inn at the Market

MAP J4 ▪ 86 Pine St ▪ 1-800-446-4484 ▪ www.innatthemarket.com ▪ $$$

This inn pampers guests in an enviable locale with sweeping mountain views. Dine at Campagne, the classic French restaurant, or at Sushi Kashiba for delectable Japanese fare.

Neighborhood Hotels

Ace Hotel

MAP H3 ▪ 2423 1st Ave ▪ (206) 448-4721 ▪ www.acehotel.com ▪ $

This hotel, located in a historic building in the heart of Belltown, appeals to guests who prefer location over luxury. There are few amenities; instead the emphasis is on the ultra-modern decor. Both Pike Place Market and Capitol Hill are nearby.

Graduate Seattle

MAP E2 ▪ 4507 Brooklyn Ave NE ▪ (206) 634-2000 ▪ www.graduatehotels.com ▪ $

An attractive choice for visiting parents, students, and professors, this award-winning hotel has designer rooms that offer comfortable beds and picturesque views of the Space Needle, the U-District, and the downtown skyline.

Inn at Queen Anne

MAP G2 ▪ 505 1st Ave N ▪ (206) 282-7357 ▪ www.innatqueenanne.com ▪ $

There is a charm and a cozy ambience that characterizes this 1930s-era inn. Rooms have kitchenettes and there is a plant-filled patio/courtyard, which is a perfect place to sip tea or coffee.

MarQueen Hotel

MAP G1 ▪ 600 Queen Anne Ave N ▪ (206) 282-7407 ▪ www.marqueen.com ▪ $

Located in lively Lower Queen Anne, this stately hotel is a short walk to the charming cafés, trendy bars, and small shops located nearby.

The Mediterranean Inn

MAP G1 ▪ 425 Queen Anne Ave N ▪ (206) 428-4700 ▪ www.mediterranean-inn.com ▪ $

Modern suites fully furnished with kitchenettes are available here. There is a fitness center, an atmospheric rooftop patio, and a secure parking garage here. The inn occupies a prime spot, right by Seattle Center.

Motif Seattle

MAP K4 ▪ 1415 5th Ave ▪ (206) 971-8000 ▪ www.destinationhotels.com ▪ $

Filled with colorful art, this hotel is a short walk from Pike Place Market, plus downtown restaurants and shopping. The rooftop patio and bar has good views of the city and waterfront.

Watertown Hotel

MAP E2 ▪ 4242 Roosevelt Way NE ▪ (206) 826-4242 ▪ www.staypineapple.com ▪ $

Primarily catering to students and their parents, Watertown boasts non-smoking premises, a seasonal pool, free parking, loaner bicycles, and a free shuttle service to select attractions.

Hotel Sorrento

MAP L4 ▪ 900 Madison St ▪ 1-800-426-1265 ▪ www.hotelsorrento.com ▪ $$

At the opulent Sorrento, guests find Seattle's finest boutique hotel as well as a destination gourmet restaurant, the Dunbar Room. Enjoy the Italian marble bathrooms, luxury linens, and a complimentary car service within the downtown area.

University Inn

MAP E2 ▪ 4140 Roosevelt Way NE ▪ (206) 632-5055 ▪ www.staypineapple.com ▪ $$

Parents and students reserve early to stay at the University Inn, only three blocks from the University of Washington. Guests can help themselves to a free continental breakfast and a courtesy shuttle to downtown.

B&Bs and Guesthouses

11th Avenue Inn

MAP M3 ▪ 121 11th Ave E ▪ 1-800-720-7161 ▪ www.11thavenueinn.com ▪ $

This quiet B&B is housed in a lovely 1906 Victorian inn. The ten guestrooms are decorated with antique furnishings and boast modern amenities. All have queen beds and bathrooms. There is free parking available.

Bacon Mansion Bed & Breakfast

MAP E4 ▪ 959 Broadway E ▪ (206) 329-1864 ▪ www.baconmansion.com ▪ $

This 1909 Edwardian Tudor mansion exudes elegance owing to its original carved wood trim, marble fireplaces, 3,000-crystal chandelier, and remarkable library.

Ballard Inn

MAP B1 ▪ 5300 Ballard Ave NW ▪ (206) 789-5011 ▪ $

Built as the American-Scandinavian Bank in 1902, this spot was converted into a hotel in the 1920s. It has 16 rooms with modern furnishings; some have shared bathrooms. The two-story building has no elevator or air conditioning.

Gaslight Inn

MAP E4 ▪ 1727 15th Ave ▪ (206) 325-3654 ▪ www.gaslight-inn.com ▪ $

Situated in Capitol Hill, this lovingly restored 19th-century inn inspires guests with its private art collection. Highlights include a heated outdoor pool, fireplaces, and stunning views. Some of the rooms have a shared bathroom.

Mildred's B&B

MAP E4 ▪ 1202 15th Ave E ▪ 1-800-327-9692 ▪ No air conditioning ▪ www.mildredsbnb.com ▪ $

This large, turreted 1890 Victorian inn takes guests back in time with lace curtains, red carpets, and a wraparound front porch perfect for lounging.

Shafer Baillie Mansion

MAP E4 ▪ 907 14th Ave E ▪ (206) 322-4654 ▪ www.sbmansion.com ▪ $

This Tudor Revival building has clean, well-appointed rooms with private bathrooms and a beautiful wood-panelled dining room. The Seattle Asian Art Museum and Volunteer Park are only a short walk away.

Greenlake Guest House

MAP D1 ▪ 7630 E Greenlake N ▪ (206) 729-8700 ▪ www.greenlakeguesthouse.com ▪ $$

Across the street from beautiful Green Lake, and close to shops and restaurants, this guesthouse has modern rooms with TVs and private bathrooms. Most rooms also have gas fireplaces.

Budget Hotels and Hostels

American Hotel

MAP L6 ▪ 520 South King Street ▪ (206) 622-5443 ▪ www.americanhotel seattle.com ▪ $

Located in the heart of the Chinatown-International District, this hotel is close to the transit and cheap food joints. Choose from a range of private rooms, some with their own bath-tubs, or hotel style bunks. There are shared kitchen and social spaces.

City Hostel Seattle

MAP H3 ▪ 2327 2nd Ave ▪ (206) 706-3255 ▪ www. thehello.com ▪ $

Award-winning budget accommodation sets this hostel above the rest. It is situated just a short walk from most tourist attractions. Local artists display their work on the walls, and movie-makers show films in the small theater. The price includes breakfast, and the use of Wi-Fi.

Green Tortoise Hostel

MAP J4 ▪ 105 Pike St ▪ (206) 340-1222 ▪ www. www.greentortoise. com ▪ $

Residing in a beautifully restored historic building, Green Tortoise has 30 bunk rooms, lockers, semi-private bathrooms, a modern kitchen, and large common areas. Free Wi-Fi, daily breakfast, and lots of activities make this a popular spot.

Hotel Hotel

MAP D2 ▪ 3515 Fremont Ave N ▪ (206) 257-4543 ▪ www.thehello.com ▪ $

This stylish hostel in Fremont offers a choice of individual rooms with private bathrooms and dorm-style rooms. Rates are inclusive of breakfast and Wi-Fi.

The Maxwell Hotel Seattle

MAP H1 ▪ 300 Roy St ▪ (866) 866-7977 ▪ www. staypineapple.com ▪ $

A pet-friendly hotel at the base of Queen Anne Hill. The Maxwell has cheerful decor that celebrates art with colorful murals, mosaics, and tiles. There are spacious rooms, an indoor pool, free bicycle use, and free parking here.

Moore Hotel

MAP J4 ▪ 1926 2nd Ave ▪ 1-800-421-5508 ▪ No air conditioning ▪ www. moorehotel.com ▪ $

This hotel features simple yet comfortable rooms, some with shared bathrooms. It enjoys a great location close to the Pike Place Market.

Panama Hotel

MAP L6 ▪ 605 S Main St ▪ (206) 223-9242 ▪ No air conditioning ▪ www. panamahotelseattle. com ▪ $

Sabro Ozasa, a Japanese architect and University of Washington graduate, built this hotel in 1910. Since then, it has housed Japanese immigrants, Alaskan fisherman, and international travelers. Rooms have sinks only, but shared bathrooms have clawfoot tubs. The staff is multilingual.

Paramount Hotel

MAP K4 ▪ 724 Pine St ▪ (206) 292-9500 ▪ www. paramounthotelseattle. com ▪ $

A charming old hotel rated among the top in the city, and good value for those who want to be in the heart of downtown. Rooms are a bit dated, but nicely furnished. There's an onsite restaurant and business center, too.

Travelodge Seattle Center

MAP J2 ▪ 200 6th Ave N ▪ (206) 962-8678 ▪ www. travelodgeseattlecenter. com ▪ $

Located near the Space Needle, this motel offers comfortable rooms, in-room coffee, and free local calls. Amenities include a seasonal outdoor pool. Basic breakfast and Wi-Fi is included in the rate.

University Motel Suites

MAP E2 ▪ 4731 12th Ave NE ▪ (206) 522-4724 ▪ www.universitymotel suites.com ▪ $

This budget option is just a few blocks from the I-5, so downtown is a quick drive away. Small suites have a living and kitchen area, a bedroom, and a full tub. There is free Wi-Fi and parking, plus laundry facilities.

Warwick Seattle Hotel

MAP J3 ▪ 401 Lenora St ▪ (206) 443-4300 ▪ www. warwickhotels.com ▪ $

This hotel is a first-rate choice for travelers who want basic amenities at much lower prices. On top of many 24-hour extras – such as room service, business and gym, and an indoor heated swimming pool – there are rooms trimmed in fine woods and marble.

For a key to hotel price categories see p116

General Index

Acknowledgments

Author
Eric Amrine

Additional contributor
Pam Mandel

Publishing Director Georgina Dee
Publisher Vivien Antwi
Design Director Phil Ormerod
Editorial Sophie Adam, Ankita Awasthi Tröger, Alice Fewery, Rachel Fox, Freddie Marriage, Alison McGill, Sally Schafer, Hollie Teague
Design Tessa Bindloss, Bhavika Mathur, Ankita Sharma
Cover Design Maxine Pedliham, Vinita Venugopal
Picture Research Susie Peachey, Ellen Root, Lucy Sienkowska
Cartography Suresh Kumar, James Macdonald, Alok Pathak, Reetu Pandey
Senior Production Editor Jason Little
Production Luca Bazzoli
Factchecker Carolyn Patten
Proofreader Laura Walker
Indexer Helen Peters
Revisions Dipika Dasgupta, Shikha Kulkarni, Rachel Laidler, Arushi Mathur, Vagisha Pushp, Priyanka Thakur, Beverly Smart, Stuti Tiwari, Vaishali Vashisht, Lisa Voormeij, Tanveer Zaidi
Commissioned Photography Scott Pitts

Picture Credits
The publisher would like to thank the following for their kind permission to reproduce their photographs:
Key: a-above; b-below/bottom; c-centre; f-far; l-left; r-right; t-top

123RF.com: Songquan Deng 86–7; Valerie Garner 61tr; palette7 4cl.
Alamy Stock Photo: David A. Barnes 90b; PhotoBliss 31bl; David Buzzard 24br; Ian G Dagnall 13br; DanitaDelimont.com / Charles Crust 63br, / Terry Eggers 2tr, 34-5b, /Connie Ricca 97tl, / Stuart Westmorland 97cr; Paul Christian Gordon 12clb, 22–3, 26c, 63tl, 80tr; Granger Historical Picture Archive 62tl; Kevin Griffin 19br; Andrew Hasson 104tr; imageBROKER / Michael Weber 71br; David L. Moore – Washington 59b; Nikreates 25tl, 78cla, 91clb; NiKreative 39tr, 70cla; North Wind Picture Archives 36t; B. O'Kane 29bl, 52br; Kevin Schafer 10br; Splash News 51tr; Mark Summerfield 98cl; UrbanTexture 29br, 93cra; Jennifer Vanderhoof 47tl; Greg Vaughn 3tl, 68–9b; Mason Vranish 79br; James Walley 81bl; We Shoot 77cr.
Bainbridge Island Museum of Art: Art Grice 49t.
Bakery Nouveau: Clare Barboza 107crb.
Camelion Design: 100tl.

Chateau Ste. Michelle: 63cl.
Chihuly Garden and Glass: Terry Rishel 14–15.
Children's Film Festival Seattle: 50tr.
Chop Suey: 54br.
Click, Design That Fits: Lisa S. Town 106t.
Dimitrou's Jazz Alley: Bruce C. Moore 54cl.
Dorling Kindersley: Frank L. Jenkins 57tr.
Dreamstime.com: Adolfolazo 107ca; Michael Albright 27bl; Anderm 14br; Andreykr 12–13; Avmedved 47br; Nilanjan Bhattacharya 4t; *Fremont Rocket* Created by John Hoge, Sculptor with Rod Miller and Jon Hegeman / photo Bizyayev 93bl; Sergii Figurnyi / Sculpture by Jonathan Borofsky 11cb, 30-31c; Blackghost600 10cl; Lembi Buchanan 7tl; Simon Campbell 55br; Josephine Celt 15tl; Crackerclips 64b; Crystal Craig 16b; Deymos 18cla; Digitalvalley 61cl; Tom Dowd 51cl; eric5 65tl; Gnives50 20-1; Esteban Martinena Guerrero 4clb, 18br; Hakoar 67cla; Hdcphoto 27crb; Mariana Ianovska 15bc; Svitlana Imnadze 46b; Jackbluee 7br, 30clb, 58bl, 42tl; Jdanne 11cra; Jerryway 42-3b; Ritu Jethani 16cra; Katinka2014 28-9c; Denise P. Lett 96cla; Richard Mcmillin 66tl; Minacarson 4crb, 13tl; Donna Nonemountry 11cr; Yooran Park 10clb; Sean Pavone 2tl, 6cla, 8-9, 27cl, 38br; Oliver Perez 49br, 74br; David Pillow 36cb; Matthew Ragen 92tl; Silvestrovairina 10cla; Kenneth Sponsler 50b; Spvvkr 89br; Angie Westre 48cla; Zrfphoto 38t, 89tr.
El Camino: 95br
Fremont Market: Matthew Sumi 88cla.
Courtesy of the Frye Art Museum: Installation view of Frye Salon, 2015. / Mark Woods 60–61b.
Garage: Steve Sonheim 85b.
Gay City, Seattle's LGBTQ Center: 82cl.
Getty Images: Philip James Corwin 19l; Richard Cummins 64cla; FilmMagic / Jim Bennett 62cla; Thomas Klinder / EyeEm 1; ML Harris 28bl; jurgita.photography 67tr; Keith Levit 23tl; John & Lisa Merrill 73cla; Michael Ochs Archives 37tr; Mona Makela Photography 98–9b; Jon Akira Yamamoto / Gamma-Rapho 31tc; Doug Wilson 37cl.
Henry Art Gallery, University of Washington: 40cla; © Martin Creed. All Rights Reserved © DACS 2017 *Work No. 360 Half the Air in a Given Space* [installation view]. 2015. Photo RJ Sánchez/ Solstream Studios. 28cla.
Hot Cakes: 101ca.
iStockphoto.com: 400tmax 17cr, 62br; carterdayne 80bl; chas272 93cr; Elementallmaging 3tr, 108–9; ndimella 4cra; njpPhoto 4b; RomanKhomlyak 66–7; twphotos 102cra.
Jive Time: 94tl.
Lark: Zack Bent 56tl.
Log House Museum: 103tc.
Metropolitan Grill: Suzi Pratt 56cb.
Moisture Festival: David Rose 92cb.

Museum of History & Industry: Kathleen Kennedy Knies 41tl.

Museum of Pop Culture: Brady Harvey 53cl.

Neumos: 55tl.

Paper Hammer: 76t.

Pike Brewing Company: Spencer Wallace 55br.

Pretty Parlor: 83t.

Seattle Art Museum: 40b; *Echo* by Jaume Plensa Seattle Olympic Sculpture Park / Benjamin Benschneider 17tl.

Seattle Children's Theatre: Denny Sternstein 14cla.

Seattle Farmers Market Association: 99tl.

Seattle Great Wheel: 71tr, Vincent Yee 10crb.

Seattle Monorail: Megan Ching 72b.

Seattle Parks and Recreation: 4cla, 103br, 104b, 105cla; Futoshi Kobayashi 25br; Laurel Mercury 44clb; TIA International Photography 11b, 32–3, 33cr, 33bl, 33tl, 46cla, 45cra, 90tr.

Seattle Theatre Group: Bob Cerelli 52tl, 53tr.

Seattle Best Tea: 22bl.

Sell Your Sole Consignment Boutique: Erica Sciareta 75cra.

Shutterstock.com: MPH Photos 74tl

Stoneburner: Geoffrey Smith 101crb.

Unicorn: Christopher Eltrich 11tl, 24–5, 79tl.

University of Washington Botanic Gardens: Copyright Stephanie Colony 60tl.

University Village: Lara Swimmer 58tr.

Victrola Coffee: 84t.

The Walrus and the Carpenter: Aaron Leitz 57bl.

Wing Luke Museum: Lindsay Kennedy 22cl.

Cover
Front and spine: **Getty Images:** Thomas Klinder / EyeEm
Back: **Alamy Stock Photo:** Inge Johnsson tr, robertharding cla, Andriana Syvanych crb; **iStockphoto.com:** Robert Meyer tl; **Getty Images:** Thomas Klinder / EyeEm b

Pull Out Map Cover
Getty Images: Thomas Klinder / EyeEm
All other images © Dorling Kindersley
For further information see: www.dkimages.com

Penguin Random House

First edition 2005

Published in Great Britain by
Dorling Kindersley Limited
DK, One Embassy Gardens, 8 Viaduct Gardens, London SW11 7BW

The authorised representative in the EEA is Dorling Kindersley Verlag GmbH. Arnulfstr. 124, 80636 Munich, Germany

Published in the United States by
DK US, 1450 Broadway, Suite 801,
New York, New York 10018, USA

Copyright © 2005, 2022
Dorling Kindersley Limited

A Penguin Random House Company

22 23 24 25 10 9 8 7 6 5 4 3 2 1

Reprinted with revisions 2007, 2009, 2011, 2013, 2015, 2018, 2020, 2022

A CIP catalog record is available from the British Library.

A catalog record for this book is available from the Library of Congress.

ISSN 1479-344X

ISBN 978-0-2415-6603-9

www.dk.com

*As a guide to abbreviations in visitor information blocks: **Adm** = admission charge; **D** = dinner.*

MIX
Paper from responsible sources
FSC™ C018179
www.fsc.org

This book was made with Forest Stewardship Council ™ certified paper – one small step in DK's commitment to a sustainable future.
For more information go to www.dk.com/our-green-pledge

Selected Street